ABUNDANT

"If I've seen anything in the life of my church community, it is that generosity is the key to happiness. Todd and his team at Generous Giving get this, and offer a fresh perspective on a topic most of us think of as laden with guilt and obligation. After reading *Abundant* you'll see why generosity is truly a pathway to living the abundant life." - **Pastor Mark Batterson, *New York Times* best-selling author of *The Circle Maker*, Lead Pastor of National Community Church**

"All too often generosity is explained in terms of how much money is given and how much good it can do. But what if we shifted the conversation to the joy generosity produces in the lives of the truly generous? In *Abundant*, Todd Harper does just that as he highlights the impact and joyfulness experienced by those who engage in the life-changing journey of living generously. As a stewardship pastor in the local church I wish every follower of Christ, no matter their financial condition, would make reading Todd's book a high priority." - **David Briggs, Central Christian Church of Arizona**

"Great read. Todd Harper unabashedly addresses the (often thought, but rarely articulated) questions that plague donors. Successfully distilling the Generous Giving conference into book form, Harper captivates the reader with his personal struggle with money and the stories of others who've discovered great joy on their journeys toward generosity. This book is a great tool to share with the person who doesn't believe it's possible to discuss generosity without strings attached." - **Martha Cimmarrusti, Trustee, Majesty Foundation**

"Todd Harper has done a superb job of inviting us to take part in an engaging and invigorating conversation that is guaranteed to give our lives more genuine fulfillment. Most impressive, Todd has been living for years what *Abundant* encourages us to embrace. I heartily recommend *Abundant*. You won't believe what you've been missing!" - **Howard Dayton, Founder, Compass - Finances God's Way**

"We are never more like Jesus than when we're giving. Generous living and giving is a response of gratitude to the grace He has so generously lavished on us. Todd Harper has a passion to see people practice grace-motivated, extravagant generosity—pouring out our resources for Christ's sake and seeing grace multiplied all round. Nothing could be more important or bring us greater joy." - **Nancy DeMoss Wolgemuth, Author, Teacher/Host, *Revive Our Hearts***

"Generosity is at the heart of God and His Great Commission. My wife, Judy, and I loved going through a Journey of Generosity with our Global Executive Team and their spouses. We look forward to partnering with Todd and Generous Giving even more! This message is important for every believer." - **Steve Douglass, President of Cru**

"Todd Harper and Generous Giving are revolutionizing the way people think about giving. This is a must-read."
- **Margaret Feinberg, Author, *Fight Back With Joy***

"No one has had more deep conversations about generosity than Todd Harper. From that wealth of experience as well as his personal journey, Todd shares stories that resonate with the Spirit in our own hearts. I love the way he explains how people of wealth are getting together in enjoyable settings to explore deep questions of faith and money—and have fun doing it! Let this new book challenge you to experience even more of the Kingdom life through an expanding adventure in generosity." - **Alan Gotthardt, Author, *The Eternity Portfolio, Illuminated***

"*Abundant* is an outstanding book that explores ways to experience greater joy, purpose, and impact through your philanthropy. Todd Harper, a leading voice in the generosity movement, weaves biblical principles with modern-day stories to present a powerful perspective on faith and wealth. Don't miss the opportunity to take part in this life-transforming conversation." - **Peter Greer, President & CEO, HOPE International, and Coauthor, *Mission Drift*.**

"In our culture today, where communication is instant and constant, a good conversation is hard to come by. I mean the kind where you are actually heard and known, a place where stories are told and life is truly lived. I've been in that type of conversation with Todd for over 17 years; he's a master of asking the right questions and willing to listen. This book is an invitation to join him in a unique conversation that I believe can be nothing short of transformational." - **Daryl Heald, Founder, Generosity Path**

"In his new book Todd does what the Apostle Paul told Timothy to do—start a conversation with the rich. At Thrivent we have learned the practice of gratitude and generosity is the prescription to an abundant mind-set (Heart), and that joyful and extravagant generosity is evidence you are on the right path to a godly relationship with money. Todd does a masterful job of having a graceful, loving, and honest conversation about the challenges and opportunities for folks that have been blessed with abundant earthly resources." - **Brad Hewitt, CEO, Thrivent Financial**

"Jesus does not call the rich to a posture of destitution, but rather, joyful distribution. Want to explore this idea further? This is the book for you! Todd Harper meets you where you are and graciously guides you from trying to maximize your net worth to maximizing kingdom impact. The best part is that you will find the journey to be the most enriching trip of your life." - **Gary G. Hoag, Ph.D. - Generosity Monk, ECFA Press Author / International Liaison**

"Generosity is such a deeply spiritual and personal topic, yet one everyone should take the time to really think it through because of the blessings available to us. Todd Harper has created a comforting, inspiring, and non-condemning book for everyone entrusted with much. Todd's stories are transparent and the way he writes makes me want to invite others to join the generosity conversation."

- **Gunnar Johnson, Executive Pastor, Pastoral Care, Equipping and Discipleship, Gateway Church**

"I picked up this book, started underlining quote after quote, and finished it in two sittings. Like a lifestyle of generosity, this book may start you on a journey to joy, freedom, and purpose." - **Patrick Johnson, Founder, GenerousChurch**

"In *Abundant*, Todd shares his own generosity journey and does a masterful job of sharing the soul of the generosity movement of which he is a leader. It is all about joy! Giving leads to greater joy! And he avoids guilt-inducing statements. This book is all about God's desire to bless those with wealth." - **Kim King, Board of Directors, Women Doing Well**

"Todd Harper has had a big part in getting the generosity conversation started among the richly blessed (or wealthy) in our country. The vision of Generous Giving to spread this message has transformed the giving practices of thousands of families. Now more than ever, we need to reach out with this life-changing message." - **Hugh O. Maclellan, Jr., The Maclellan Foundation**

"The counterintuitive story that it is more blessed to give than to receive, lives vibrantly through this book. Consider it an invitation to step into the greatest adventure of your life." - **Pamela Pugh, Founder, Women Doing Well Initiatives**

"*Abundant* is a book about joy! And Todd Harper is an experienced guide. This book lets you be a fly on the wall in a room you probably didn't know existed. Read it and you'll overhear the rumblings of a quiet and almost invisible movement happening in our day. Read it and you'll discover the road less traveled, but find in the end it was the true pathway to joy." - **John Rinehart, Author, *Gospel Patrons* & Founder, gospelpatrons.org**

"Todd Harper embodies the spirit of joy that the Apostle Paul extols in his beautiful letter to the Philippians. Enthusiastic joy-generator that he is, Todd is magnificently affirming in this important, must-read meditation on wealth. The Parable of the Talents confirms in Christ's teachings what we innately sense through our nature as humans created in the image of God—Christians do well when they perform brilliantly with their God-given gifts and talents and then find themselves, by God's grace and their own hard work, at the pinnacle of the ladder of success. Todd invites the most successful among us to reflect on their unfolding, or perhaps nearly complete, journey of energetic and productive talent-utilization, and at the same time gently invites us to become all that God wants each of us to be—generous givers who care deeply and lovingly about a hurting world. Like our Lord's parables themselves, Todd's biblical insight is simple but powerful—by caringly giving, we create joy in human hearts, beginning with our own."
- **Ken Starr, Former Solicitor General of the United States**

"Having watched Todd, and his wife Collynn, lead remarkably generous lives for the last 30 years, I can attest that there are few people that can speak to this subject in such a genuine way. This book is as inspiring as it is practical, which makes it a must read!"
- **David Wills, President, National Christian Foundation**

"Over the years I have been personally challenged and inspired by Todd Harper and his team. I have enthusiastically recommended Generous Giving to the pastors and churches that I serve and Generous Giving has served those churches well. Now I am happy to recommend that my friends in pastoral ministry share a copy of Todd's book with their members who have been entrusted with much." - **Chris Willard, Generosity Strategist with Leadership Network and Generis, Coauthor,** *Contagious Generosity, Creating a Culture of Giving in Your Church*

"As one of the founding members of the Redeemer Stewardship Committee in New York City, I see this book as a catalyst to ignite a generous culture in major urban centers. Read this book, host a JOG, and be part of a Kingdom adventure you've only dreamed about." - **Janice Worth, President, Anushka Inc.**

ABUNDANT

EXPERIENCING THE INCREDIBLE
JOURNEY OF GENEROSITY

TODD HARPER

FOREWORD BY RANDY ALCORN

DEDICATION

To Collynn, my wonderful partner in life, parenting, and ministry for twenty-eight years. I know of no one more committed to giving her life away for the sake of others.

To the Trustees of the Maclellan Foundation, whose vision and generosity have enabled the unique conversations we've been having for the past fifteen years.

To the amazing Board, Team, and Volunteers at Generous Giving that I have the privilege of working with every day. I am humbled to be associated with such talented and generous people.

ACKNOWLEDGMENTS

Daryl Heald, David Wills, and Forrest Reinhardt are to be primarily credited with this book. This is their story as much as it is mine. They were the cofounders of Generous Giving and have been critical to its ongoing growth and development.

Randy Alcorn, whose writing inspired and changed each of the founders of Generous Giving. I am grateful for his ongoing encouragement and clear voice on the power of generosity to shape our hearts.

Lyn Cryderman, whose giftedness as an organizer of ideas and as a writer made this project possible. It has been a delight to work together. You made this fun!

Thank you to every volunteer who has joined us to live and share this message. You have made the principles of God's Word compelling and attractive as you live your lives.

CONTENTS

FOREWORD

In 1989 I wrote my first book on financial steward-ship, *Money, Possessions, and Eternity*. Since then I've updated that book and have written *The Treasure Principle* and *Managing God's Money*. Giving is a topic I'm passionate about. I consider it part of my life's calling to encourage God's people to have an eternal perspective when it comes to their finances. That's why I'm delighted to write the foreword to this book.

I first met Todd Harper in the late 1990s along with Daryl Heald, David Wills, and Forrest Reinhardt, the other founders of Generous Giving. To this day I deeply appreciate all of these leaders. I had the privilege of speaking at the first several Generous Giving confer-ences, and saw the ministry close-up in its infancy. Since then I've spoken at a half dozen other Generous Giving gatherings. I've also been part of a Journey of Generosity in a private home. I love the Generous Giving organiza-tion, and it's been gratifying to see its impact go deep and wide.

This movement resonates with every fiber of my being. Glorifying God in how we use our money isn't a duty; it's a delight! Giving brings great happiness, and our happy God rejoices when our hearts celebrate. In the only statement of Jesus in the book of Acts that's not in the Gospels, Jesus said, "It is more blessed [*makarios*, happy-making] to give than to receive" (Acts 20:35). Yet too many believers never experience the overwhelming grace of God, which is the lightning that produces in our lives the thunder of giving, and a joy unlike any other.

To many, Todd Harper is the primary face and voice of Generous Giving. As president, he loves communicating a Christ-centered and joy-cultivating approach to giving. I've been with him in many places over the years and have seen him at work. Todd genuinely loves people and views them not as a means to the end of funding good causes, but as those whom God has created and gifted who can use encouragement in the journey. This book is a reflection of Todd's heart and values.

In *Abundant* Todd explores the challenges of wealth, deeply familiar to him through his years of working with successful leaders and their families. He provides a plan to help break down the isolation and confusion that so often accompany material wealth. Through engaging in honest, low-pressure conversations, believers often discover they're not alone in their struggle to grow in generosity. This is one of the most attractive aspects of Generous Giving, and it comes through in this book.

As someone who has never served in an official capacity with the ministry, but who has seen it firsthand since its beginning, I can say without question that God has used Generous Giving, and continues to do so under Todd's leadership, to reach people with a vitalizing message that has forever changed families, churches, and the work of Christ around the globe. As a facilitator of deep, heartfelt, and joyful conversations about giving, this ministry helps people discover that God's plan for their money can be liberating and full of happiness!

Todd and the Generous Giving team have cultivated a culture in which hundreds of business leaders worldwide own the mission of Generous Giving, which is to spread the biblical message of stewardship in order to grow generous givers among those whom God has entrusted with much wealth. Hence, Generous Giving is growing through volunteers, rather than paid staff members. More Journey of Generosity retreats held each year are completely volunteer-hosted and volunteer-led, with peers engaging their peers, exploring God's purposes for wealth through open and invigorating conversation. This isn't simply one person's message—it's a powerful and beautiful movement of the Holy Spirit among His people.

Abundant invites you to take a closer look at this movement. The book is refreshing, engaging, and personal. Todd's warmth allows the reader to be challenged without being threatened.

I long for Christ's kingdom work to be funded at greater levels, but I long just as much for God's people to experience the radical life-changing joy of giving done as an act of love for Jesus and others. May God continue to use this ministry, and use this book also, to that end.

Randy Alcorn
Director, Eternal Perspective Ministries
Author of *Money, Possessions, and Eternity,*
The Treasure Principle, Heaven, and *Happiness*

ONE

It's Okay That You're Wealthy

Take a deep breath and relax. I'm going to talk about money. Your money. More specifically, I'm going to talk about the relatively small (but growing) number of people in America who have a lot of money. For example, we now have approximately ten million millionaires in America, more than at any time in our history. Approximately 142,000 households in the United States are worth more than $25 million. And billionaires? More than 2,000 in the world, with the United States leading the way with 536.

I'm assuming that you're holding this book because you are one of those fortunate people who have been blessed with a significant amount of money. I'm not going to scold you for being wealthy. Shame you for taking nice vacations. Or blame you for global poverty. So let's get that out in the open. God has blessed you financially and that's okay.

I fully understand if you're a little nervous—even suspicious—when it comes to hearing what someone like me might say about your money. You have become an easy target. Politicians and pundits seem to take great pleasure in showcasing the lifestyles of America's wealthiest, implying or directly declaring that rich people are selfish, greedy, and insensitive to the needs of others. Well-meaning preachers and authors quote statistics about how Christians give such a small portion of their money to the church. And then there are those in the public eye who flaunt their wealth in such a way that it tends to paint all rich people with the same brush: all you care about is yourself and your toys.

I don't believe that for a second.

For most of my career, I have had the opportunity to work closely with a lot of wealthy people, and here's what I have discovered: I like you! Most of you worked hard to get where you are today, often starting with very little but persevering in a tough, competitive business climate. Some of you inherited your wealth but have managed it well. The vast majority of you understand that all that you have comes from God, and you desire to be good stewards of what he has given you. Are there some bad apples in the basket of wealthy people? Of course, but overall—and especially among believers—wealthy people care about others and often support causes that make the world a better place.

What I have also learned from getting to know wealthy people is that you possess a growing awareness that having a lot of money isn't the easiest thing in the world. Here are some of the thoughts and questions that come up when I talk with my wealthy friends:

- What about our kids? How do we enjoy our lifestyle without spoiling them?
- When we can afford just about anything, how do we decide what to buy?
- What are we losing in all this gaining?
- I know money doesn't equal happiness, but I thought I'd be a lot happier once I reached a certain level.
- Every time the pastor preaches on stewardship, I feel like he's got me in his crosshairs. Am I just paranoid?
- You probably think I'm crazy, but I actually worry about losing it all someday.
- I want to trust people, but I'm not sure who to trust.
- Sometimes I wonder if anyone likes me for who I am, or just for what I have.
- Is it possible to reclaim that innocence and freedom we experienced when we were just starting out and still have what we have?
- Who can we talk to about the challenges and opportunities of wealth?

It's easy for the rest of us to think that if we had your wealth, life would be easy. But I do not recall any of my wealthy friends telling me that the larger their net worth, the easier it gets.

And for good reason. The kind of wealth I'm talking about—and that I assume you are experiencing—is a relatively new phenomenon. Eric D. Beinhocker, whom *Fortune* magazine named as Business Leader of the Next Century, claims that ninety-eight percent of the wealth that exists today was gained over the past 250 years.[1]

No wonder we're just now learning how to handle all of this.

Then there's the whole "one-percenter" issue, as if there's something wrong with you for having a household income that places you in the top one percent of the U.S. population. But here's another way to look at one-percenters: globally, those whose household incomes exceed $38,800 annually represent one percent of the world's wealthiest people. Which means the majority of us in America have been richly blessed.

Rich people have been around for a long time, but not *this* rich or *this* many. For example, prior to 1790, the concept of a millionaire was unknown in America. Most citizens in the new nation were happy to have just enough—having more than enough meant a few extra dollars to buy a new horse or expand your garden. Savings usually meant a few bills stuffed into a sock and hidden under your mattress. The New York Stock Exchange would not get off the ground until 1792, and the first bank had just been ordered into existence by the fledgling Congress. Of course, a few fortunate citizens had a lot of money, but nothing close to what we are experiencing today. Then John Jacob Astor began exporting furs to Europe, and by 1800 he was worth

---

[1] Eric D. Beinhocker, *The Origin of Wealth* (Boston: Harvard Business Review Press, 2006).

$250,000—about $5 million by today's standards. From one millionaire in 1800 to ten million today. By historical standards, that's not a lot of time or critical mass to figure out what to do with all that money.

Don't get me wrong. There's a lot of information about how to make money, how to invest it wisely, and how to make it work for you. Most of you have accountants, financial planners, brokers, and advisors to help you get the most out of your money. Even in the faith community, resources abound that offer biblical perspectives on money. So it's not like you're clueless about being wise and conscientious with your wealth.

So why another book about money?

Because a lot of wealthy believers just like you are having an honest and invigorating conversation about their wealth, and I'd like you to join it. I hope to introduce you to a quiet, almost invisible movement that is going on among those entrusted with much. People who love God, are active in the church, and desire to be good stewards of their time, talent, and treasure.

People like Alan Barnhart, who grew the family business from a small mom-and-pop outfit with ten employees to a $400 million global company with one thousand employees, and found himself wondering what to do with a fortune he couldn't possibly spend in his lifetime. Or Renee Lockey, a doctor who decided to live on a nurse's income. Or countless other followers of Christ who have been blessed with great wealth and have found a safe venue to talk about it with each other. These people don't have it all figured out but are benefiting from conversations they are having, and that's what this book is about. How to experience the abundant life by engaging in conversations with others like yourself. How to ensure that your entire life is as abundant as your net worth.

One such conversation began in the late 1990s around a table with three of my friends who, like me, had been observing what was going on with wealthy Christians. If you recall, the 1990s marked the beginning of an explosion of personal wealth in the United States. The stock markets were burgeoning. The ascent of the high-tech industry was accelerating. People were becoming multi-millionaires overnight. The four of us were in a variety of positions that allowed us front-row seats to observe what was happening in the world of philanthropy. On the one hand, we were encouraged to see evidence of generosity among many wealthy people. And yet, overall, giving in America was lower than what it had been during the Great Depression. In other words, the economic conditions between then and the 1990s couldn't have been more different. But at one of America's lowest points economically, people gave more as a percentage of income to charitable organizations. And it's not getting any better. Giving as a percentage of GDP in 1933 was three percent; today it is two percent. So despite the recovery and growth of the economy, giving has declined steadily for eighty years.

So we began meeting to try and figure out what was going on, why so many people—not just the wealthy— were holding onto their money, and why a handful of others were exceedingly generous. While all this wealth was being created, the global church was exploding.

From an economic perspective, people were trying to figure out how to fund innovation through the tech revolution. From a kingdom perspective, we saw this as an opportunity to find ways to fund the incredible growth in the body of Christ globally.

The fact that giving in general had been in decline for eighty years was distressing, but that really wasn't the primary focus of our conversation. Each of us was interacting with a handful of people who were exceptionally generous, and we wanted to learn what set them apart—what led them to hold onto their wealth so loosely. And it wasn't just that they gave of their wealth so generously. They also seemed to be having more fun than anyone we had ever encountered, living lives of meaning, purpose, and joy. Was there a connection? That's what we wanted to find out.

Around this time, I attended a screening of the *Jesus* film that the organization I worked for, Campus Crusade for Christ (now known as Cru), has shown all over the world. A man by the name of Hugh Maclellan spoke at this event and shared how he consistently gives away seventy percent of his annual income. This was the first person I had ever met who actually gave more than he held onto. Earlier in my life, I had read about R. G. LeTourneau, who lived on ten percent of his income and gave the rest of it away. But this was the first time I actually had met someone who lived this way, and it rocked my world.

Even though my job was to raise money from wealthy donors for Cru, I never asked Hugh Maclellan for money. Instead, I brought people to Hugh so they could meet him, play golf with him, hear his story, and see what he was like. And that's when I realized that we don't need to tell people they should give more money to God's work. All we need to do is invite them to join the conversation.

That's what we will be doing throughout this book—having a conversation. I'm not going to ask you for a penny. I'm not going to pressure you into moving your giving from one level to another. Rather, I will expose you to a conversation where many are finding great joy in investing more generously in God's kingdom. By sharing from their wealth that they believe really belongs to God in the first place, they are experiencing the abundant life that Jesus promised: "I have come so that they may have life, and that they may have it more abundantly" (John 10:10, KJV).

In many ways, this book is about more than just money. Which is ironic. Because from as early as I can remember, all I ever wanted was to be rich.

TWO

Money: My Love Affair

I don't understand it and can't explain it, but I have always loved money. I loved making it. Counting it. Spending it. And whenever I spent it, I replenished the supply by making more.

Christmas 1977. My aunt's and grandmother's traditional Christmas gift to me and my four siblings was fifty dollars. My siblings each got a card with a fifty-dollar bill inside. Not me. My card was a little bigger and stuffed inside were fifty one-dollar bills. Why? It was no secret to everyone in my family: even at ten years old, I loved to count money.

Somewhere in my house is an old picture of me taken at one of my middle school birthday parties. It's of a poster one of my relatives made for me. My name is spelled out in dollar bills.

Yep. Not only was I obsessed with money, but everyone around me knew about it. I suppose that made it easy for them when it came time for gift-giving: "If you want to make Todd happy, give him money."

I grew up in a home that economists would call an "upper-middle-class" family. My dad had a good job as an executive with an oil company, and we lived in a comfortable house in a nice neighborhood. But we clearly weren't rich, and to my chagrin, I learned why. When I was about thirteen years old, my mom related a story to me about my dad. At the time the story took place, I was about three years old, and my dad's boss took a real interest in him. The conversation between my dad and his boss went something like this:

Boss: "I really like what I see in you, Harper. You could have a bright future here, but I'd like to see you spend more time at the office."

Dad: "That's very kind of you, sir, but my family comes first."

When my mom shared that story with me, I was crushed. Disappointed. All I remember thinking was, "You mean we could have been rich?"

Of course by global standards, we and just about every American were rich. I didn't really need anything because my parents adequately provided for us. Except that I loved stuff, and despite being cared for so well, I always wanted more. Money for me was a way to get the stuff I wanted, and I wanted a lot. I learned that if I wanted something that my parents wouldn't buy me, I had to find a way to buy it myself, and so from as far back as I can remember, I found ways to make money. I got my first paper route when I was nine years old. When I was eleven years old, I started mowing lawns. By the time I was in high school, I was mowing eighty lawns a week and earning $1,000 weekly during the growing season in Naperville, Illinois. I've never had so much disposable income!

In the winter, I ran a snowplowing business to keep my cash flowing. But that wasn't enough to fund the buying of all the stuff I wanted: cars, ski equipment, stereos, clothes, etc. Every winter, I bought brand-new ski equipment—skis, boots, poles, the latest ski gear. I bought my first car when I was sixteen years old—a one-year-old Chevy Chevette with all the options. Where other kids usually looked for used bargains, my stuff had to be brand new, brand name. In fact, my nickname throughout high school was "Top-of-the-Line Todd." I hated that nickname, but it accurately described me.

As I went off to college, I branched out into a different money-making opportunity. I began buying and selling utility trailers. It went like this. I needed a trailer to haul my lawn-mowing equipment around, but they were pretty expensive in the Chicago area. I discovered they were much cheaper in Texas, so I would drive there, pick one up, then drive back to Naperville and sell it for a profit. Eventually I bought a much bigger trailer so I could load it up with three or four trailers, thus reducing the overall delivery cost of each trailer.

That experience of buying low and selling high led to another "job." By the time I was eighteen I had obtained my Series 7 securities license. By passing the Series 7 exam, I was qualified to trade all types of securities on the New York Stock Exchange. So as a young college student, I was already a licensed stockbroker.

I suppose every kid likes to have a little money. Looking back, I took it to a pretty ridiculous level. But to me, it didn't seem unusual or obsessive at all. It just made sense. If you wanted something, you could get it. You just had to work for it. As a registered stockbroker, you might assume that I invested a lot of the money I was earning. Not exactly. In fact, I invested very little. Instead, I spent most of what I earned. When most kids head off to college, if they're lucky they might hit campus in a rusty old beater of a car handed down from a relative. I paid cash for a brand-new Z-28 Camaro on my way to college.

Even my choice of colleges was motivated by my love for money and the things it could buy. At the time, Baylor University was one of three colleges in the United States that offered a degree in entrepreneurship, so off to Baylor I went.

Considering the way I was so driven by money, you might conclude that I grew up in a family that was either completely lacking in faith or only nominally Christian. But the truth is, I grew up in a wonderful Christian home. We attended a Bible church, and my parents were the type that showed up whenever the doors of the church were open. Both were actively involved, and it rubbed off on me as well. At the age of seven, at my mother's prompting, I made a decision to accept Christ. And even as I fed my materialistic lifestyle, I, too, was active in church and never once really thought about the relationship of my faith with my money. In fact, in the evangelical world of my family and friends, I was sort of celebrated as this young entrepreneur who wasn't afraid of a little hard work in order to make some money. And I didn't just work hard for money. In middle school, I became one of the student leaders of our little youth group. All eight of us. By the time I graduated from high school, that little youth group had grown to more than three hundred students who met at the church every Wednesday night.

To everyone around me in church, I was the embodiment of the Protestant work ethic. Hard work pays off with money, which is a blessing from the Lord. What's not to like about that? I wasn't lazy. I wasn't spoiled. I did well in school and was active in church. And if I wanted something, I didn't beg for it—I worked hard until I had enough money to buy it. No one ever cautioned me about maybe liking money too much.

Well, almost no one.

I don't remember all the details, but one day while I was in high school, my mom handed me a book and casually mentioned that she thought I would enjoy reading it. I didn't know it at the time, but I suspect now that this was her way of addressing something she saw in me that concerned her. The book, *Mover of Men and Mountains*, was the autobiography of R. G. LeTourneau, the legendary Texas manufacturer of earthmoving equipment. I began reading it right away, and by the time I finished it, I was marked forever.

Part of the appeal, I think, was that as a young man, LeTourneau began making money by working hard at whatever odd job he could find. I could relate to that. His early ability to make money may have been the hook that got me into the book, but what really kept my attention was how instead of just using his money to buy things, he gave most of it away. For the first time in my young life, I came face-to-face with an idea that was completely foreign to me: the creation of wealth for the benefit of others. Naturally I was familiar with the biblical concept of tithing, and I dutifully calculated ten percent of my week's earnings to put into the offering plate at church. But here was a guy who at the time was the world's most famous individual in the heavy equipment business. Owner of more than three hundred patents, with construction plants scattered over four continents. Seventy percent of the heavy earthmoving equipment used by the Allied Forces in World War II came from his factories. Immensely wealthy, he lived on a fraction of his income so that he could help others. If I thought my dad was crazy for turning down an opportunity to move rapidly up his company's corporate ladder, this guy must have been certifiably nuts. Except he wasn't. And I couldn't get that out of my mind.

In my little teenaged head, money was all about how I could use it for myself. Yes, I gave my tithe to the church, but only because I was taught that Christians were supposed to do that. And to be honest, it was hard. I struggled with it. I was not what the Bible calls a "cheerful giver." Why in the world would someone give a penny more than he had to?

I'd like to report that reading that book changed my life, and I started giving a lot more than my ten percent. It didn't. I kept making as much money as I could so that I could buy whatever I wanted. Which ultimately led to that shiny red Camaro that took me to Baylor University, and that's where I learned that for every Camaro there's a faster and fancier BMW. This drive for the best might never end.

It's also where I learned that the best wasn't exactly what I thought it was.

THREE

What's Your Plan?

When I left Naperville and headed south to Waco, Texas—home of Baylor University—I had one primary goal in mind: to become a millionaire by the age of thirty. I already knew how to make money; Baylor would help me learn how to make lots more. Its Hankamer School of Business produced highly respected leaders like American Airlines CEO Thomas Horton, Oracle Corporation CEO Mark Hurd, and one-time Houston Astros owner Drayton McLane Jr. My plan was to go through their entrepreneurial program, graduate, and put all that newfound business savvy into starting a company that would make me rich.

It was a good plan, and it might have worked if I had not gone to Sunday school.

A lot of Christian kids temporarily or permanently ditch their faith when they go away to college. And even though Baylor's roots run deep into the Southern Baptist

Convention—it's the largest Baptist university in the world—it offered plenty of opportunities to wander from the fold. You're away from home, parties aren't hard to find, and nobody's checking to make sure you go to church.

In spite of that freedom, I went to church. Specifically to Highland Baptist where I joined a popular Sunday school class for college students taught by Dr. Jamie Lash, one of Baylor's economics professors. He called the class "The Victory Seminar," and the essence of the class was based on Jesus' words in John 8:31-32: "If you hold to my teaching, you are really my disciples. Then you will know the truth, and the truth will set you free." On one of the first Sundays I attended, the professor shared a simple illustration that I will never forget and that began a change in me that continues to this day.

> Write down on a piece of paper what you hope would be the best plan for your life. Who you'll marry, where you'll live, what kind of work you'll do. Let yourself dream big and create the perfect plan for your life. Now, if you could see God's plan for your life written down on a separate sheet of paper, you'd tear up your silly little plan in a heartbeat.

Shortly after hearing that illustration, I went on a fall retreat sponsored by Cru. We arrived Friday night at a camp out in the country near Midlothian, Texas, and on Saturday morning we were given a full hour to find some quiet place and spend time with the Lord. I grabbed my sleeping bag, found a spot in a field, and lay on the ground, staring up at the sky. In that hour I had the most real conversation with God that I had ever had in my life. To this day, that conversation remains crystal clear in my memory.

As a slight breeze whispered across the field, I clearly sensed God asking me, "Do you believe I am who I say I am? Do you believe that I am the Creator of the world and therefore the Creator of you, and if so, do you believe I know what's best for you? Or do you need to hold onto your own plans for your life?"

Following that Sunday school class, it became clear that God was essentially drawing a line in the sand for me. Am I in or am I out? Not in terms of salvation, because I had settled that a long time ago. This was a lordship question. My plan was all set. I wanted to be a millionaire, and that's why I was at Baylor. But as I lay there in a grassy meadow in Midlothian, Texas, I told God I would do whatever he wanted me to do. I decided that day that I wanted what he wanted for my life, not what I wanted. I had no idea what that meant in terms of career plans. All I knew was that I had just surrendered everything to him, including—and maybe especially— my plan to become a millionaire.

I got up from that spot and noticed another guy about a hundred yards away from me, and for whatever reason I decided to head over and introduce myself. His name was David Wills, and he seemed like an okay guy. So okay that we've been close friends for thirty years. In fact, he's one of the three guys who joined me in this conversation about wealth, and here's where my story begins to interact with yours.

I continued my studies at Baylor, interrupted by another great decision—marrying my wife, Collynn, which led to yet another interruption. We took a year off after my junior year and served as missionaries with Cru in Romania, which was then part of the Soviet Bloc. We would be sharing the gospel behind the Iron Curtain where atheism was the official "religion." My wife was thrilled because she felt called to be a missionary. I, not so much, but there was that decision I made to follow God no matter what.

We returned to Baylor the following year where I graduated with a degree in entrepreneurship and economics, and then after some training with Cru, we moved to Russia. It was thrilling to introduce Jesus to people who had never heard of him, but I also continued to exercise my entrepreneurial talents by buying real estate there and investing carefully. To be honest, I wanted to be a rich missionary. I still read *The Economist, The Wall Street Journal,* and *Businessweek*. And then my friend David Wills sent me the book *Money, Possessions, and Eternity,* by Randy Alcorn. It sort of smacked me upside the head, explaining that I had it all backwards. Here I was investing in stocks because I wanted to be rich, but in his winsome, inviting way, Randy helped me see that I was still holding on to my plan. It seemed like a good plan, just not the *best* plan. I thought of giving to the kingdom as an obligation, but he showed me how giving was something we *get* to do, not *have* to do. Through his exposition of Scripture, Randy showed me a radical version of generosity that is done for the good of others, and ultimately for my own good. It shifted my investment horizon from thirty years to thirty million years.

We returned to the States after four years, and I began raising money for Cru. As much as I believed in what Cru was doing around the world, I started to have questions about my calling. If all I was doing was shifting peoples' resources from, say, Navigators to Cru, I was not adding any value to the kingdom. Of course, I had Randy Alcorn's book rattling around in the back of my head. I also had Paul's writing in Philippians 4 about not being interested in what's credited to my account but what is credited to God's account. I realized that if I was going to stay in this space of asking for money, my calling had to be broader than just representing a worthy cause. If I could help people find ways to lay up more treasure in heaven, then that was a worthy calling. If I couldn't do that, I would be better off going into business and creating wealth on my own so I could do so.

It was with that mind-set that I began a conversation with David Wills along with two other guys I had met who were, like me, involved in some aspect of funding Christian ministry. By that time, David was the president of the National Christian Foundation. Daryl Heald served as a Senior Grants Manager for the Maclellan Foundation, and Forrest Reinhardt worked as the stewardship pastor with Rick Warren, pastor of Saddleback Community Church.

We shared a passion for helping Christians get beyond the sense of obligation or duty when it comes to giving. How could we help more people experience the liberating joy of generosity? In the beginning, we had no strategy or plan, but sort of stumbled our way forward with a shared vision of what we wanted for people. For example, in the early 1990s, the Maclellan Foundation had produced a series of tapes about strategic giving, so we convinced them to update them. Instead of recording the speakers in a studio, we decided to do it in front of an audience. So we brought in all the stewardship heavy-weights, invited about a hundred friends to a nice venue, and then added something a little different. We invited Scott Lewis, a very generous giver to Christian minis-tries, to share his story, and it turned out that Scott's story stole the show.

We learned from that experience that the best way to encourage generosity is to tell stories and facilitate a con-versation. The biblically based teaching was wonderful and certainly helpful, but what was different for people was talking with their peers about questions revolving around having a lot of money.

So we put together a proposal for a grant from the Maclellan Foundation that went something like this: "We want to invite people to a weekend event held in a comfortable place so they can talk about generosity. We want to provide world-class speakers who will offer bib-lical perspectives about wealth. And we want to offer tes-timonies from wealthy Christians who are somewhere on the journey toward becoming cheerful givers. Oh, and we are adamant about this one little detail: we will never ask for money. We simply want to provide a safe place where they can learn about the joys of generosity."

They didn't come right out and say it, but the trustees at the Maclellan Foundation were skeptical. They didn't think it would work, primarily because when they fund an initiative, they want to be able to measure its success. If we didn't end the event with a pitch for more money to various ministries, how would we know if we're doing any good?

We tried to explain that what we were after was more transformational than transactional. We wanted to help people answer the "Why should I be generous?" question. Funding the kingdom has traditionally meant convincing a donor to give to a particular ministry. We felt that if we could create an environment that could transform people's thinking about their resources, the rest would take care of itself. Or as I sometimes tell people, "We don't ask for anything, but Jesus asks for everything." Andy Stanley puts it this way: this was something we wanted *for* them, not *from* them.

That initial effort in 1999 became what we now call Generous Giving. Today we organize a national conference called the Celebration of Generosity, as well as hundreds of intimate retreats or Journeys of Generosity, all with one purpose: to explore the biblical message of generosity and engage in a conversation with like-minded Christians about how that message liberates us. We never ask for money, a feature that no one really believes until they actually come to one of our events. One of the most common responses we hear from attendees is, "I kept waiting for that big appeal at the end of the event, or a follow-up mailing asking us to contribute, but it never came."

And it never will.

We believe this conversation is more important

now than it ever was, and we'd love to have you join in. Remember, it's okay to be wealthy. I have zero interest in "guilting" you into giving more money to your church or any other ministry. But I do want you to experience the joy that thousands of others have gained from this ongoing conversation. Because this liberating truth is the best inoculation against a dangerous message from the culture in which we live, do business, and raise our families.

FOUR

The Culture of More

Because of your wealth, you are a target. Some have you in their crosshairs so they can attack you for being a "one-percenter." Others hit you up with requests to donate to their causes. But there's another more subtle predator stalking you, and its only weapon is a message. A nearly irresistible appeal: "Bigger, better, faster makes you happy." It's what sells Ferraris, penthouses, yachts, Gulfstreams, and Armani. As I've mentioned before, nice things aren't necessarily bad. The conversation I want you to join is intended to inspire you, not condemn you.

One of my dear friends who has been blessed with substantial wealth once said to me, "I read *The Wall Street Journal* every day, and on every other page I read that evocative message you always talk about—bigger, better, faster will make me happy. My problem is that I can afford it all. So what's the grid that I can use to decide whether or not to buy what they're selling? It all looks pretty nice." For people of modest wealth, those decisions are pretty much determined by their income. They may still be vulnerable to the message—we all want to be happy, right? But they are limited in what they purchase because they can only afford so much. You, on the other hand, can have it all. Or at least a lot of it. And in our culture, more is truly seen as better.

My friend is a devoted follower of Christ. He wants to be obedient, to be a good steward. But he inherently knows that he is vulnerable in the "culture of more" in which he lives, and that its effects are so subtle that he may not even be aware of what's happening to him. And although we're focusing on people like you who have so much, this is a universal issue for most Christians living in affluent cultures such as ours. Even in my own life, when I read the Bible—especially the words of Jesus—my culture informs how I read and interpret what he says.

For example, Jesus very clearly says, "Do not store up for yourselves treasures on earth" (Matthew 6:19). And because I live in a culture where financial security is practically a right, I think to myself, "Surely Jesus doesn't mean I shouldn't save up for retirement." Why would I think like that? Watch one hour of television in the evening, and count how many commercials warn you that you might not have enough money to live more than a few years beyond retirement. Pick up *Time* magazine or *Businessweek* and note the prevalence of investment firms suggesting your retirement is at risk if you don't sign up with them. The Bible, as evangelist Billy Graham used to observe, never mentions retirement. This is a cultural phenomenon that has been so ingrained in our thinking that I cannot read that passage warning about storing up treasure without thinking a little defensively about retirement. My culture affects how I read and respond to God's Word.

The Bible also teaches us to pray for our daily bread (Matthew 6:11). And not to be anxious about tomorrow because God will take care of us tomorrow (Matthew 6:34). Jesus seems to be saying I don't need to save up a lot of money for the future, but I have been so conditioned by the advice of financial planners that it seems absolutely foolish not to keep contributing to my IRA.

I'm not suggesting we shouldn't responsibly prepare for the future. And I could probably make a strong case about how the New Testament was written in a different time and place where the economy was primitive and unlike our own complex system. Or that we need to balance this teaching with others that implore us to care for our families and loved ones (1 Timothy 5:8). But the fact remains—the culture in which we live heavily influences the way we read and respond to God's Word. And one of the most consistent and dominant messages of culture is that you need a lot more than what you currently have, and once you get it you will finally be happy.

If you're like me, you are probably thinking, "I know that my happiness only comes from the Lord, so thank goodness I'm inoculated against that false message from culture." I've yet to meet a wealthy Christian who believes a designer watch on his wrist will make him happy. But I've met more than one Christian with a designer watch. Madison Avenue doesn't care if we believe the message or not. Only that we act on it. And it shouldn't surprise us that we do. The false message from our "culture of more" is not only insidious and subtle, but relentless. Companies spend billions of dollars to generate desire. You listen to that message and see it on flashy billboards on the morning drive. If you read *Fortune, Inc., Entrepreneur, Travel,* or other periodicals that know you can buy just about anything, you can't escape that message of more. Your iPhone, iPad, and laptop quickly learn enough about you to target that message even more specifically to your desires.

Even if we are immune to those efforts to generate desire, there's yet another way that our culture shapes our thinking, and that's through our friends. This happens at every socio-economic level, and it goes like this: You pull into the church parking lot and notice that one of your good friends from your small group is driving a new car. And it's gorgeous. You congratulate him and he shows you its features, and you're happy for him, and you're just two buddies appreciating a new car. But on your way home from church, you're thinking it might be time to buy a new car. And not just *another* new car, but a bit of an upgrade. Your current ride is fine. Until you see your buddy's new car.

When this happens to me, it's not a matter of coveting or trying to keep up with the neighbors. When they buy a nicer car, vacation at a better resort, send their kid to a prestigious college, it's only natural to at least kick the tires, so to speak. Why wouldn't I want my son to get a great education? Or to treat my family to a fabulous vacation?

Again, there's nothing wrong with nice things and experiences. If you drive a Lexus, vacation on Lake Como, or drop your kid off at Harvard, you're not a bad person. All of us must choose how to negotiate a culture that dangles bigger and better in front of us wherever we turn. What many of us in this conversation are learning, however, is that while having more is not in and of itself wrong, the message behind it is. How you survive in this culture hinges on your expectations. In other words, what really constitutes "the good life"?

The culture in which we find ourselves would have us believe that the way to happiness is to gain more. More money. More things. More pleasure. As followers of Christ, we inherently know that true abundance comes only from God, yet we are still vulnerable to the culture of more and its powerful pull on our lives. My wealthy friend who acknowledged he could have it all was really struggling with questions like, "How much is enough?" and "What really is the abundant life?"

One of the subtexts of the "culture of more" is that religion—especially Christianity—is a barrier to your happiness. That it's a bunch of rules designed to take all the fun out of life. The Bible, on the other hand, teaches that obeying God and following his teaching is the only way to experience not just the good life, but the best life. Consider this exhortation from the Apostle Paul in his letter to Timothy:

> *Command those who are rich in this present world not*
> *to be arrogant nor to put their hope in wealth, which*
> *is so uncertain, but to put their hope in God, who*
> *richly provides us with everything for our enjoyment.*
> *Command them to do good, to be rich in good deeds,*
> *and to be generous and willing to share. In this way*
> *they will lay up treasure for themselves as a firm*
> *foundation for the coming age, so that they may take*
> *hold of the life that is truly life.* 1 Timothy 6:17-19

Life that is truly life. The "more" that we crave is only available to those who put their hope and trust fully in God. This is not a criticism of wealth or the nice things it can buy, but a reminder that the happiness we seek will never be found in "more," but only in a God who wants to lavish us with his blessings: "For I know the plans I have for you," declares the Lord, "plans to prosper you and not to harm you, plans to give you hope and a future" (Jeremiah 29:11).

What I have learned from being part of this conversation with wealthy Christians is that the "grid" to help you navigate your way through this "culture of more" is to place your complete trust in God's Word. That may sound overly simplistic, so think of it this way. On the one hand, you have a multi-billion dollar machine whose only goal is to generate desire. And it does this by promising that your next acquisition will make you happier. On the other hand, you have a God who does not condemn you for being wealthy but invites you to place your trust in him and not in the things you are buying. Which of those two messages rings true to you?

Or to put it another way, how long did the "happiness" last after you bought that new _____ (fill in the blank)? I love the smell of a new car, and for the first few weeks, I can't wait to hop in and drive it to work. But in a relatively short time, it almost turns on me and becomes just a car. It gets me to work. And back. Not exactly my idea of happiness.

Many of the people who are having this conversation about wealth have decided to take God at his word. I have watched people downsize their lifestyles in order to be more generous, and always with unexpected delight. I've seen friends sell large homes and move into smaller ones and find that there's greater intimacy with their children because they are physically closer to them. I've observed others divest themselves of properties and other resources only to discover more energy for relationships. They didn't know the cost that having so much was extracting from them.

Alternatively, I've seen families buy larger homes in order to practice their gift of hospitality. I've seen friends begin to use their airplanes as tools for ministry. The conversation is not necessarily about living on less; it is about how to align our lifestyles with God's unique call on our lives.

This may be where you decide to stop reading.

But truly, this is not about what you get rid of or what you keep. This conversation is not about things. It's about experiencing the abundance that God wants for you. The money that you have earned can be a source of great joy or a burden that can lead to tremendous disappointment. Fortunately, we have a reliable resource to help us enjoy the former and avoid the latter.

FIVE

The Bible and Money

If you're not sure how to manage your money, there's no shortage of resources available to help you. Tax accountants can help you avoid paying more taxes than necessary. Investment companies such as Morgan Stanley, Merrill Lynch, and Goldman Sachs provide a variety of investment products and counsel on which ones would be best for you. According to the U.S. Bureau of Labor Statistics, there are 223,400 financial planners in the United States,[2] all willing and able to help you make wise money decisions. And then there's your broker, your cousin who seems to always pick the right stocks at the right time, and of course, a variety of financial media in print, on television, and on the Internet.

Those resources are all great, but I'd like you to consider a different type of guide that's even better, more

[2] See http://www.bls.gov/ooh/business-and-financial/personal-financial-advisors.htm.

reliable, and more trustworthy. Of course, I'm talking about the Bible.

Remember that day when as a college student I decided to believe that God is who he says he is? I also had to decide if I believed the Bible. I mean really believed it enough to trust its wisdom over any other source.

As I engage in this invigorating conversation with wealthy Christians, inevitably the "Bible question" comes up, and it goes something like this: "I try to live my life according to God's instructions in the Bible, but when it comes to my money, I'm a little hesitant. I mean, do I really have to sell all I have and give to the poor?"

When we began this conversation with wealthy Christians, we agreed that everything had to be grounded on the authority of God's Word. In essence what we were trying to do was illustrate biblical principles with modern-day examples. Real people who have a lot of money, who have decided to completely trust whatever God said about money, and how that's working for them. We wanted to explore what would happen if rich Christians put their complete trust in what the Bible teaches about money. We started out with the tagline "Experience the joy," but after some time we changed it to "Finding a joy unexpected." Because what we observed is that when people decide to trust the Bible with their money, they aren't really sure what will happen. Some even approach it with a little skepticism. But always, those who sign on for this adventure do not regret it. They have more fun in ways they had never imagined possible. In fact, one of the most confirming signs I have observed in all the years I've been working with wealthy Christians is the fruit that is produced in the lives of generous Christians.

I've never met an unhappy generous person, and if we truly believe the Bible, that shouldn't surprise us. One of the most frequently quoted Bible verses about money comes straight from the mouth of Jesus: "It is more blessed to give than to receive" (Acts 20:35). The word "blessed" sounds pretty high and holy, but the actual Greek word from which it was translated means "to make happy." In other words, "It is more happy-making to give . . ." And in my experience I cannot think of a single example where this has not proven to be true.

But that's just one verse. There are more than twenty-three hundred verses in the Bible about money. Jesus spoke more about money than any other topic. He said more about money than about heaven or hell. There's more written in the Bible about money than written about prayer and faith combined. Clearly money is a big deal to God, so the question all of us who love him have to address is, "Do I really believe what the Bible teaches about money, and if so, what am I going to do about it?"

So what does the Bible actually say about money? Lots. But its message could be summarized with a couple of simple sentences: Be careful. Be generous. Be careful because earthly success could equal spiritual failure, a warning Jesus offers in the Parable of the Rich Fool (Luke 12:21). The best way to be careful is to hold your money loosely—be generous. And that's where we focus most of our attention when we bring wealthy people together to have a conversation about money.

We don't ask them for money. We don't challenge them to increase their giving by a certain amount. Instead, we talk about generosity. What does it mean? What does it look like? What does it do for others? What does it do for us? How does it shape our hearts? How does it influence our appetite for things eternal?

The foundation for our conversation about generosity rests on the following six core messages from the Bible:

Giving Brings Joy

Remembering the words the Lord Jesus himself said: "It is more blessed to give than to receive." Acts 20:35

I have seen this message validated over and over again in the lives of generous Christians. It is the "unexpected delight" that always results when someone decides to live generously. And while our focus is usually on money, this message also applies to giving your time or talent away. At one of our larger events in Colorado Springs recently, a guy who had built a successful construction company shared how he used to view giving somewhat legalistically.

"I always gave my ten percent to the church, sort of like checking off a list of things to do," he explained. "I can't say I got all that excited about it. But once I grasped the concept of generosity, giving became fun. My wife told me she had never seen me write a check before with a smile on my face."

He's experiencing that transition I describe as moving from "I ought to give" to "I get to give."

Another guy at that same event shared how every

now and then, just for the fun of it, he'll pay for the groceries of the person in front of him at the grocery store checkout.

"Sometimes I honestly sense God is telling me to make that lady's day, but truthfully, the reactions I get make *my* day!" he said.

Contrary to the message of popular culture that religion—specifically Christianity—takes all the fun out of life, Jesus offers a life that is not dependent upon wealth for happiness or pleasure. The truly abundant life that comes from obeying God has little to do with more stuff and everything to do with more freedom, peace, joy, adventure, and purpose.

Giving Is a Heart Issue

For where your treasure is, there your heart will be also. Matthew 6:21

As I referenced earlier, I have been profoundly influenced by the writing of best-selling author Randy Alcorn. He advises, "If you want a heart for something, invest in it." And to illustrate he explains that if you invest in Google, you get more interested in news about Google. You follow it closely. There are lots of other tech companies, but you're more concerned about Google because you've invested in it.

Similarly, if you invest in the kingdom of God, your heart grows for the things of the kingdom. Giving generously leads to increased spiritual growth and vitality. You become the recipient of your own giving. This may be why the Bible has more to say about money than prayer. Conventional wisdom suggests that if you want a closer relationship with God and a stronger, more dynamic faith, you need to spend more time in prayer. I wouldn't dispute that other than to say that the generous Christians I am privileged to know seem to also enjoy a fulfilling and deepening relationship with Christ.

God Gave First

> *For God so loved the world that he gave his one and only Son.* John 3:16

God gave his Son, Jesus, who then gave his life for us. This is the ultimate example of generosity, and we are called to bear the image of God in all that we do. We, then, are most like God when we are generous.

Why is this message so important to us? Because being generous is not something you do simply because I suggested you do it, or your pastor told you to do it, or the vice president of development from a worldwide ministry asked you to do it. Our motivation for being generous springs from our desire to be more like God, to follow his example, especially when he has given so much to us.

The Apostle Paul writes, "You will be made rich in every way so that you can be generous on every occasion, and . . . your generosity will result in thanksgiving to God" (2 Corinthians 9:11).[3] Is it possible that God has allowed you to be successful financially so that you can "be generous on every occasion"?

---

[3] Read more of the Apostle Paul's teaching on Christian giving in 2 Corinthians 9:6-15.

Seek First God's Kingdom

But seek first his kingdom and his righteousness,
and all these things will be given to you as well.
Matthew 6:33

As an older commercial for an insurance company stated, life comes at you hard. In our fragile economy, anything can happen. The market drops by a few points, and some people lose millions of dollars. A serious illness can eat through savings in the blink of an eye. While the number of millionaires in the United States has increased steadily, so has the number of bankruptcies. It is in that uncertain context that Jesus calmly reassures us: "Make me your priority, and I will take care of you."

What's most important to you? That's your priority. It can only be one thing. A priority is something that is more important to you than anything else and needs to be dealt with first. Most Christians would say that Jesus is more important to them than anything else. It's pretty easy to say, but in our conversation we emphasize this message because so much is at stake. Earlier in Matthew, Jesus teaches that we can't serve both God and money, then adds this curious instruction: "Therefore I tell you, do not worry about your life" (Matthew 6:25).

It's difficult to be generous if we worry about things, especially money. Conversely, if God and his ways are more important to us than anything else, we can be generous and not worry that we'll run out of "all these things." We have to be careful here. This is a promise about life, not about material wealth. Jesus is not telling us that if we give, we get more money in return. Rather, generosity

produces the virtues of joy, peace, purpose, and contentment that give life true meaning. At the same time, many
of the people who have joined our conversation have significantly increased their generosity, yet I do not recall a
single instance where anyone ran out of money because
he or she gave too much away. But suppose someone did.
Suppose he gave every penny away and his account hit
zero. According to this promise, God will take care of him.

Do we really believe the Bible? Can we trust it? How
do we move into greater levels of trust? I have a feeling
you'd love to join that conversation.

God Owns It All

The earth is the LORD's, and everything in it.
Psalm 24:1

Imagine working for a large foundation with near-
unlimited resources. Your job is to give your foundation's
money away to causes that it has decided to support.
One day you might deliver a $10 million dollar check to
a university. Another day you hand a $2.5 million check
to a neighborhood center that provides job training for
teenagers. What a great job! You get to give to all these
wonderful causes and institutions, spending someone
else's money.

If you're a Christian, you've probably heard "God
owns it all" hundreds of times, usually when the pastor
preaches about stewardship. You may have even said it a
few times yourself when a fellow believer alludes to your
wealth: "Well, God owns it all. I'm just a steward." But
what does that really mean?

It means when you are generous, you're really giving away someone else's money. That's what makes it fun. Truly generous people understand that they are God's money managers. Their wealth is not really theirs. Instead, they know that God has entrusted us with his resources so that we can use them as he directs. When we understand this biblical message, we become like that guy who hands out checks for the foundation. What a great job! I don't have to worry about sharing "my" money, because it really isn't mine. It all belongs to God.

Heaven Is My Home

> But our citizenship is in heaven. And we eagerly await a Savior from there, the Lord Jesus Christ.
> Philippians 3:20

You've likely seen the illustration that Randy Alcorn and others have used to remind us our time on earth is brief, yet life in heaven continues forever. Draw a line across a piece of paper, then go back and make a dot with the tip of your pen or pencil just above the beginning of the line. The dot represents your time here on earth. Seventy, eighty, maybe ninety years. Seems like a long time, especially when you're in your thirties or forties. But compared to the line—eternity—it's barely a nano-second. As Randy directs so succinctly and poignantly, "Live for the line, not for the dot."

Living for the line means that our primary focus is on what we can take with us, not on what will be left behind. All the money and the things that we buy stay. Who we truly are as children of God is all that we take with us so that we can enjoy a relationship with God forever. So why spend so much time on things that are temporary? Why not spend more time on drawing closer to God, becoming who he created and blessed with gifts and financial resources? Or to put it another way, if heaven is our true home, why worry about the furniture, appliances, and landscaping that we can't take with us?

Generosity keeps us focused on what really matters, what really is important to God. When we are generous in Christ's name, we are furnishing our eternal home with treasures far greater than anything we can buy on earth. That doesn't mean spending money on nice things is wrong. It just might not be the best option, and certainly not the only option. Because in our heart's true home none of that will matter.

The Bible says a lot more about money, but these six foundational messages sufficiently guide this conversation that is happening among a growing number of wealthy Christians. I have watched thousands of people just like you apply them to the way they manage their money, and always the results exceed their wildest dreams. Not specifically because they are more generous, but because the Bible is true and can be completely trusted.

When we believe and act on that, we understand what more really means.

The *Real* Culture of More

Allof us want more, and that's not necessarily bad. I love my family and covet more time with them. I like a nice bowl of apple cobbler, and when I'm finished I'm tempted to scoop out just a little more. And they must put some secret chemical in chips and salsa because I can never stop at just one handful. I want more. When I look at my investments, I never think, "Gee, I hope they haven't given me too big of a return this month." It's natural to want more of the good things in life and less of the bad. The challenge is to understand the "more" that truly satisfies, and then learn how to obtain it. Most of the more we want only offers temporary contentment. When we bring affluent people together, this is one of the topics that often turns the conversation inward: "What is the more that I truly desire, and how do I get it?"

As followers of Christ, our heart's desire is to be more like the Savior we follow. To love God, obey him, trust him. I can't think of anyone who is a part of this conversation who would not affirm this desire to more consistently live as Jesus instructed us to live. That, plus the knowledge that their wealth could interfere with that desire, is what brings them into the conversation. Perhaps this young dentist described it best. As he sat with four other couples around a table in a lovely ballroom at the Broadmoor Hotel in Colorado Springs, he shared, "My highest priority is to serve God with everything that he has given me, but it's hard. I have a successful practice. I make a lot of money, which enables me to enjoy a lifestyle that I never had growing up. I just want to find the right balance between enjoying the good things in life without losing sight of what God expects from me."

I love his honesty. Can you imagine being that transparent with a group of Christians? What we've learned over the years is that most affluent people are reluctant to talk openly with fellow believers about their finances because they think it may sound arrogant or insensitive. But when they come together with other Christians who have been blessed financially, they get right to the heart of the issue. And in the dentist's case—as with so many—the heart of the issue is more: "How do I find the more that I'm looking for?"

Just to be clear, this question is not restricted to wealthy individuals. All of us want more, regardless of income or net worth. And all of us learn at some point that the more we have been pursuing eventually loses its ability to satisfy. We also have a pretty good idea of what it takes to experience the more that Jesus offers, and that's where many of us struggle. In the "upside-down" kingdom of God, the only way to obtain the more that we desire is to surrender. It's counterintuitive. All our lives we've been taught that if we want more we have to go out and get it. Work for it. Build. Grow. Achieve. That's likely how you have increased your own wealth. But that's not how we obtain the abundant life that God offers us.

The real "culture of more" is a place of surrender rather than conquest. It is offering all that we are, all that we possess, and all that we desire to God's purposes and then watching him direct our paths in ways that we never could have dreamed. On paper, that sounds like what every Christian is supposed to say. In reality, it can be scary. Often, the idea of surrender can feel like losing. Similarly, the thought of giving God ownership of everything can feel careless. Experiencing the "culture of more," then, is really a matter of trust. Can we trust God to do what he says he will do? Is he really capable of giving us "immeasurably more than all we ask or imagine" (Ephesians 3:20)?

The "culture of more" that surrounds us is measured in net worth, square feet, horsepower, carats, clients, accounts, ROI, IRR, acquisitions, gallons, barrels, and bushels. All of which are vulnerable to bad decisions, fickle markets, and other forces often beyond our control.

The *real* "culture of more" is so vast it can't be measured, and it lasts forever.

If that's the case, why do so many people hesitate to

surrender everything to God? And for that matter, what does surrendering even mean?

These are great questions, and all the more reason for you to join us in this invigorating conversation. But for now, I'll try to answer with a story or two.

In 1857, twenty-year-old Thomas Maclellan surrendered his life to God by making the following covenant:

> I renounce all former lords that have had
> dominion over me and consecrate all that I am
> and all that I have, the faculties of my mind, the
> members of my body, my worldly possessions,
> my time, and my influence over others, all to be
> used for Thy glory and resolutely employed in
> obedience to Thy commands as long as Thou
> continuest me in life. . . . Use me, O Lord, I
> beseech Thee as an instrument for Thy service.
> May I bring some avenue of praise to Thee, and
> of benefit to the world in which I dwell.[4]

Eventually Maclellan became a successful banker, only to see his bank fail, losing all his own money as well as the money of those who had accounts with his bank. Undaunted, at an age when most men would retire, he began selling books door-to-door in order to provide for his family and repay all who had lost money when his bank failed. Once he got back on his feet, he purchased an insurance company in Tennessee that provided disability policies for people in high-risk professions who could

[4] See http://www.maclellan.net/cms/covenant.

not obtain insurance from traditional insurers. He also promised to pay all just claims within a week—a policy unheard of with most companies. He kept this promise, even when he had to dip into his own salary. At about this time, he renewed his covenant with God, surrendering everything in his life and only asking for the privilege to serve others in God's name.

Understanding the human tendency to live only for ourselves, Maclellan made that covenant in 1857, renewed it in 1887, and renewed it again in 1907 when he wrote:

And I humbly desire Thy blessing as I now would renew these former covenants and add this fresh expression of my faith in Thee as my Triune covenant God, and of my desire to be enabled to be more Christ-like in heart and life. Oh! That Thou wouldst bless me indeed—me and mine—now and in the future, here and hereafter.[5]

Today, we know Maclellan's insurance company as Unum, one of the largest insurance companies in the world. Five generations after Maclellan made his covenant with God, his family continues the essence of his devotion to God, giving tens of millions of dollars annually to advance God's kingdom.

If Thomas Maclellan could speak to us today, he would likely tell us with great conviction that we can trust God to do what he says. And that the "more" that

---

[5] See http://www.maclellan.net/cms/covenant.

resulted from that covenant surpassed the more he received from all his business success. That's the abundance that Christ promises us when we obey him.

Because that happened so long ago, you might question whether a person could make such a covenant in today's complex economy. People can and still do, and I was privileged to see one example up close and personal.

For a number of years, I worked with an international organization known as Cru, begun in 1951 as Campus Crusade for Christ by Bill Bright, a young businessman, and his wife, Vonette. Cru has been responsible for introducing millions of people to Christ in the United States and around the world.

As a young businessman in Hollywood, Bill had little interest in God or the church, but through a series of circumstances he began attending a church where he was introduced to Christ. Shortly after that experience, he married Vonette, an Oklahoma girl he had known since she was very young. Two years into their marriage, he made an unusual business decision.

"The Lord impressed us to surrender everything to him," he told me a few years before he died in 2003. "So we wrote out a contract signing everything over to God—I'd never heard of this being done, but as a businessman I thought that was the best way to do it."

The day after signing that contract, Bill explained that God gave him a vision for the world that eventually became Cru.

"In my opinion, if there had been no contract, there would have been no vision," he said. "God brought us to the place where we made total, absolute, irrevocable surrender, and then he knew he could trust us. And from a practical point of view, we have learned that we can trust him as well. When he led us to start this ministry, we knew he would guide us. We view ourselves as a suit of clothes for Jesus. If we love and obey him, he does the rest."

When you surrender you give up control, and that can be scary. Vonette recalled that when they made this decision, she told God that she would at least like to have a modest home. Bill admits that prior to signing that contract, material things meant everything to him.

"But now God had given us a different standard," he said. "Instead of laying up treasures on earth for ourselves, he showed us we should lay up treasures in heaven."

Vonette added, "But all along, God has provided everything we have needed. We have never wanted for anything for very long."

At the time of my interview with the Brights, Bill and Vonette's combined salary from Cru—a global ministry with a budget just under a half billion dollars—was $65,000.

Are Thomas Maclellan and Bill Bright unique? In terms of the scope of their influence, perhaps, but their stories sound very much like the stories I hear often from those in this conversation about wealth and God. One aspect of my job that I enjoy the most is watching entrepreneurs, business owners, and other wealthy individuals change what they're solving for. Typically, in the business world we solve for maximizing net worth. Start a company, grow it in value, and sell it. We call it a liquidity event. Many people in business orient their lives in that way. What is most exciting for me is to watch someone change from maximizing net worth to maximizing kingdom impact. When that shift begins, the real "culture of more" is introduced into these people's lives, and they always report that orienting their lives for kingdom impact is infinitely more exciting than adding another zero to their net worth.

That's what happened to my friend from high school, Tim Mohns. Tim loves the Lord, is an elder in his church, has a beautiful wife, two great kids, and a successful financial planning business. But as he told his wife, Rachelle, one day, "If this is the American Dream, America can keep it. I don't want it."

Tim was bored.

Ironically, our organization, Generous Giving, was becoming a growing movement, and Tim was one of three guys I had been thinking about inviting to join our team. He listed all the reasons why he didn't think he could accept my offer, most of them related to having to downsize and live on a smaller income. So I asked him to do two things: one, prayerfully put himself in a position of surrender before God, and two, attend our next Celebration of Generosity event, which was to be held in Portland, Oregon. Tim and Rachelle followed through on both requests, showing up at our event in Portland where they listened to stories from people just like them, and they initially thought, as Tim later told me, "These people are nuts." But as he got to know others who were enjoying the adventure of generosity, he noticed one thing they all seemed to have in common: "They were some of the happiest people I'd ever met in my life."

For a guy who was bored with his storybook lifestyle, meeting these people intrigued him.

> I thought I had reached Nirvana when it came to my life as a successful Christian businessman. I tithed regularly. I was active in my church. I'm a generous guy. And then I met all these generous people and realized I can't go to work for Generous Giving because I'm not a generous person. The question of lifestyle and money made so much noise in my life that I couldn't even contemplate what these people were doing. And then Randy Alcorn spoke and told us that God prospers us not to increase our standard of living but to increase our standard of giving. That was a radically different way of thinking for me.

Tim and Rachelle returned to their home in suburban Chicago and decided to cap his salary to what it would be if he worked for us, and then give the excess away. It turned out to be such an exhilarating experience that they have continued living on their modest salary so that they can give generously to kingdom ministries. He never came to work with Generous Giving, but he's enjoying a new sense of purpose and calling in his current profession.

"I love living like we're living. Now we are freer financially than we have ever been—even through the downturn in the financial markets. I understand more clearly today what I'm being saved from. All from taking this adventure in generosity."

Tim discovered that the real culture of more is not about money or possessions, but about the abundant life Jesus offers when we put our complete trust in him.

So what about you? Are you bored? Do you find yourself drawn to these stories? I know you love the Lord and are serving him, but would you describe your current life as adventurous? Exciting? Abundant? At the same time, are you a little skeptical? Wondering what really goes on at these events where people like you come together to talk about money, faith, God's grace, and generosity?

In a way, I feel like the advertisers on those infomercials: "For just $19.99 you and your spouse can attend a Journey of Generosity and be changed forever!"

Except it's not $19.99. It's free. And here's what you can expect.

SEVEN

You're Safe Here

The guests begin arriving around noon and check into their rooms. Earlier, I drove over from Orlando to Longboat Key to get in eighteen holes with Chris and Susan, who are hosting this weekend's Journey of Generosity, or JOG. Chris has lined up a few unoccupied condos in his building for the five couples who are joining us. If you have not been to Longboat Key in January, you're missing an absolutely stunning destination for golf, tennis, long walks on the beach, fabulous sunsets, exquisite dining, or just sitting on your balcony overlooking the Gulf and taking it all in. That's sort of the point. We want our guests to feel almost as if they're on a vacation or a quick getaway from the busyness of their lives, and Chris and Susan's beachside resort offers that and more.

After attending one of our annual Celebration of Generosity events, Chris and Susan decided to host one of these smaller, more intimate conversations. Semi-retired and enjoying the adventure of generosity, they felt led to invite a few of their friends who they thought would enjoy talking about faith and money in the relaxed surroundings of the resort and their nicely appointed condos. In 2015, Generous Giving volunteers hosted more than two hundred Journeys of Generosity. A JOG is an overnight retreat focused on the joy of living generously. It includes stories of generous givers, interactive discussions, reflection opportunities, and Bible study. All in a period of just under twenty-four hours.

The goal is as deliberate as it is simple. Bring like-minded people together in a pleasant setting. Encourage everyone to join in lively, meaningful discussion during five sessions led by a trained facilitator. Set aside time for prayerful reflection. Provide opportunity for some fun. We do this over parts of two days, starting at 2:00 p.m. the first day and ending at noon the next. People are busy. Many have kids at home. An overnighter seems to fit everyone's schedule, yet still gives us time to dig into God's Word and each other's thinking.

Often, everyone already knows each other since the host couple generally invites friends from church or business relationships. But even if that's not the case, it's never long before the conversation and laughter flow freely. It's almost as if people are eager to get after this topic because they know they are in a safe environment. Unlike many traditional small groups, in a JOG everyone understands that they aren't the only people in the room blessed with financial wealth, so that "stigma" is off the table right from the start.

We also stick to a few ground rules to ensure a safe, productive environment. Turn off cell phones. Try not to give advice. Agree to confidentiality. Participate but don't dominate. And even before people agree to attend, we let them know that other than transportation, everything is free. And they will never be asked for money. Really!

Around 1:30 p.m., twelve of us are standing around Chris's spacious kitchen drinking coffee or juice, sampling an array of fruit, pastries, and desserts. The atmosphere is relaxed, with a fresh breeze blowing in from the ocean through the open sliders leading out to the expansive balcony. It feels more like a prelude to a barbecue instead of a guided conversation about money. Without any fanfare or formal announcement, the "party" slowly moves into the living room, as this particular JOG is about to begin.

And we always begin with a story.

In fact, if Scripture is the foundation of every JOG, stories are the walls, windows, and roof. Who doesn't love a good story? Besides, that's how Jesus taught. By telling stories. The Gospels contain lots of stories but only one sermon from Jesus. Over the years we have collected a treasure of stories communicated beautifully through professional video crews—stories of other affluent Christians who have begun the journey and have already witnessed amazing things that they never imagined possible. (Feel free to peruse any of our stories in our media library at generousgiving.org.)

As the facilitator, I try to push the right keys on my laptop to get the video up on Chris's wide-screen television, and we always start with the same one: "Miracle in

Franklin." I won't give away the plot, but the reason we always lead with this story is because it so beautifully captures the essence of what a JOG is all about: it is more happy-making to give than to receive.

The subtext of the video—and of generosity—is joy. For so many Christians—especially Christians blessed with wealth—money, giving, tithing, and stewardship are often wrapped in a variety of fairly negative emotions. Organizations send us pictures of starving children, and even though we feel compassionate and want to help, we also feel a little guilty. Tithing is often unintentionally presented as an obligation. And as a financially successful person, you've obviously heard all the criticisms directed at wealthy people. The JOG attempts to counter this negativity or skepticism with biblical truth: generosity produces joy.

As the video ends, I look out across the living room and see smiles. Even a smile or two through tears. I also sense some relief, as if they're thinking, "Maybe this is actually going to be fun." Even though in most cases everyone knows each other, we spend the next several minutes introducing ourselves, but with a twist.

"In addition to giving us your name," I begin, "I'd like you to tell us why you came and then share a significant memory from before you were twelve years old that you think might have influenced your view of money or giving."

You know how sometimes in small groups there's an awkward silence after the leader asks people to respond? Not this time. In fact, what happens next sets the tone for this particular JOG, and mirrors what usually happens at these events: there is no shortage of conversation. A wife shares how she grew up dirt poor and never forgot the time when someone from church stopped by at Christmas with a box full of gifts. A husband recounts how his dad stressed saving for a rainy day, and how to this day he always makes sure he has enough in case his business or the economy tanks. Another guy remembers how his parents supported missionaries even when their personal finances were tight. After one couple shares individually, they both look at each other and almost speak simultaneously: "I've never heard that story before." I could let this go on for hours, as each story ignites even more memories that others want to jump back in and share. As often happens at a JOG when people share, I have to call "Time!"

I scroll down the menu on my laptop and start the next video. Best-selling author and New York City pastor, Tim Keller. What we try to do in our brief time together is move back and forth from head to heart. In Tim's video, which is an excerpt from a sermon on Acts 20:35, he raises a question that generates a lot of discussion: What do you spend your money on *effortlessly*? It's a tough question because it can uncover a quality in us that we don't want to acknowledge: greed. But rather than condemn people for being greedy, Tim confesses his own greed by admitting that the target of his effortless spending is books. Nothing wrong with books, but for Tim, they can become an idol as he finds his identity in being a smart and gifted teacher rather than in being a child loved by God.

It's funny how a highly respected Christian leader's

admission of greed and idolatry breaks down our efforts of trying to look respectable to each other. When I first contemplated his question, I thought my answer was family vacations—the more exotic the better. But that was really just my "Gee, that's not so bad" answer. In reality, I have come to see that what I spend money on effortlessly is my savings account. Please understand—I've always viewed saving money as a good thing. But for me it can become an obsession and reveals a deeper truth: I can easily place my security in money rather than God.

Just as before, the conversation is lively and transparent. I'm supposed to facilitate, but most of the time I sit and marvel at how eager our guests are to talk about how they spend their money, about how they have never connected their spending habits with what they truly treasure. I look at my watch and realize it's time for this session to end. Like the middle school teacher trying to get the class to quiet down, I have to raise my voice a little and announce it's time for our afternoon break. I remind them that there are refreshments in the kitchen and that our second session will begin in twenty minutes.

Almost reluctantly, a few leave their seats and head into the kitchen. A few more remain seated. But all are still talking. About money. About that family in Franklin, Tennessee. About whether spending money on something you really like is a matter of enjoying God's gifts or revealing what you truly treasure.

The journey has begun for this small group of friends. Each is beginning to understand just where he or she is in the adventure. I make a mental note to remind them when we reconvene that on this journey, no one arrives. Chris and Susan, our hosts, have been at this longer than the rest and they would be the first to say they're still learning. That it's still fun. That they're not bored. For some, this is the first time they have ever talked so openly with others about how they think about and relate to their money. For others, it is the first time they have talked about these issues so openly with their own spouses. Yet no one is heading for the exits. I couldn't stop this conversation if I wanted to. And I don't want to.

This is the conversation I've been talking about. Ordinary believers just like you who have been blessed with wealth and are having a blast figuring out how God wants them to use it for his kingdom. Even as you read this, the conversation continues. In other JOGs. In the kitchen after the kids head off to school and a mom and dad talk excitedly about a project they'd like to support. On the golf course as a couple of JOG alums talk more about generosity than work. We've seen marriages deepen. Families clarify their purpose. Individuals find meaning, contentment, and joy. All because of a simple conversation.

You know how when you go to a work conference or business meeting, and at break time everyone checks their phones for messages or places a couple of calls before they have to get back to work? Not here. Not today.

I stroll into the kitchen and grab a yogurt and some granola. Session Two begins in five minutes, and you won't want to miss it.

EIGHT

What Does Generosity Look Like?

Generosity is one of those words that's difficult to define, but you know it when you see it. When you go to a restaurant and your server brings you a plate piled high with food, you sometimes refer to that as a generous portion. Do you give a generous tip? If so, what's generous? Twenty percent? Thirty percent? Have you ever been around someone who seems to look for opportunities to give you a verbal pat on the back? That person is generous with his praise.

When we all get back together for Session Two, our goal is to understand what generosity looks like. And one of the best ways to do that is to look at a story like the one involving Pete and Deb Ochs. (Search "Pete and Deb Generous Giving" on the web, or locate their video in our media library at generousgiving.org.)

Growing up in a farming family in Kansas, Pete became an entrepreneur, purchasing businesses, running them wisely, treating his employees fairly, and giving a tithe of his wealth back to God.

"Although both Deb and I grew up in generous families, I was a 90-10 kind of guy," Pete explains. "In fact, my goal was to make a lot of money so that ten percent was a big number. But you can imagine what I had planned for the ninety percent."

It wasn't until he came under the influence of a couple of mentors that he understood the concept of stewardship:

"As stewards, we're really only managers. We don't own anything. When you understand that, it puts a whole new spin on how you live your life. For one thing, it causes you to begin thinking, how much is enough? Regardless of how much money I make, how much do I really need to live?"

Pete began hanging out with some other entrepreneurs who were struggling with that same question. They all were making a lot of money and intuitively knew that money could be their downfall. So they did something unconventional. They agreed to help set each other's salaries and gave each other permission to define what they would spend on themselves, revisiting this process annually. Talk about accountability.

"We pretty much tell each other how much money we should keep for ourselves, and the rest goes to others," Pete continues. "All of us could be taking home a lot more money than we do, but this was our way of answering the question, 'how much is enough?'"

Pete and Deb have given the concept of generosity a lot of thought, adopting an acrostic from the word L-I-F-E:

Be generous with your *labor*, be generous with your *influence*, be generous with your *finances*, and be generous with your *expertise*. Pete began to look at the businesses he owned as resources God had given him. How could he use them not only to create financial capital, but to create social capital and spiritual capital as well?

So he went to prison.

"Several years ago I purchased a commercial seating business that was somewhat labor intensive, yet a fairly straightforward process where we could use some of the technology from our other businesses," Pete explains. "Why not take this business into a prison as a way to help some of society's worst criminals by employing them?"

When he says worst, he's not exaggerating. His employees include guys serving life for murder, and when they heard what Pete wanted to do, they thought he was crazy.

"I told them I wanted to make their prison the best prison in the world, and they looked at me like I was nuts," Pete laughs.

In addition to learning skills that could be put to use when they got out, Pete offered them a class in life skills that met every two weeks. The men learned how to be better fathers, how to deal with difficult relationships, how to manage money, and other lessons they would need to become productive citizens. He also challenged them with the concept of generosity, offered to match them dollar for dollar whatever they donated from their prison wages, and gave them a list of charities they could support.

"It's amazing how much money these prisoners donated," Pete says, "and what's really neat is most of the charities they chose were to help victims of crimes they committed."

For Pete, this endeavor is about more than investing his money in a business that happens to operate in a prison.

"Pete's been to our living area," one inmate recalls. "No volunteer has ever done that. He's come to church with us inside and is very involved in our lives. It's clear that he has a desire to see us succeed."

Would Pete and Deb be changing men's lives in prison if they hadn't decided to cap their income so they could be more generous? Tough question, but my sense is that if he was still a 90-10 guy, that ninety percent might have prevented him from doing something to help serious criminals.

"It really goes to the faith issue," Deb explains. "We do for others because Christ has done so much for us."

When I share this video story with the group, I ask what stood out to them as they watched it.

"When he's in the prison workshop with the prisoners, he looks like he's having fun," one observes.

"There's something different in the lives of that couple that's palpable, and it's something I want more of in my own life," another confides.

"Those prisoners in the video don't fit my stereotype, but maybe it's because they've been given meaningful work to do," says another.

And finally, "That part about capping your income? Pretty scary."

This last observation may be the most important because you can't have a genuine conversation if certain things are off-limits. We never ask JOG participants to share their specifics of income or net worth, but we create an environment where people can talk honestly about the challenges they face as wealthy Christians. And it's when someone admits something is "scary" that others begin to open up:

"I like the idea of setting a limit, but I'm not sure I want someone else to know what that is."

"I agree, but then if we really believe we don't own anything—that we're just stewards—why should we care?"

"What do you do if you set a limit and then spend it all, and you've got three more months to go?"

Everyone laughs.

You might think I'm being disingenuous, but that's really our goal. Not to arrive at some conclusion where everyone has to agree, but to provide an opportunity for a conversation. Not everyone will arrive at the same destination, but all will benefit from the conversation they are having while on the journey. What's happening is that all participants are beginning to think about generosity that's outside the norm—that goes beyond writing a check or increasing their giving to a certain percentage.

Since we believe the Bible should be the foundation for our conversation, I give them an assignment: "Turn to page five in the workbook we gave you earlier today. You'll find a passage of Scripture—2 Corinthians 9:6-15. Take twenty minutes to read it, and then ask yourselves three questions: "What does this passage say? What is God telling *me* in this passage? What is my response?"

You may recognize this as a simple "inductive Bible study" method. This method is based on the idea that the Bible isn't just an ancient document, but God's inspired words directed to each of us, and if we read it carefully and deliberately, we'll hear those words in our own context. In this passage in 2 Corinthians, the Apostle Paul is helping a group of Christians in the city of Corinth move from giving as an obligation to generosity as a way of life. If you get a chance, read it as a letter directly from God to you. Better yet, find a JOG and do this inductive Bible study with other people who are wrestling with issues surrounding their material wealth. I'll tell you how in Chapter 12, but you can always go to our website (generousgiving.org) to learn more about these conversations.

Not one of us in Chris's living room is a trained theologian or Bible scholar, but each person shares insights that make this passage come alive in ways that many of us have never experienced before. For example, one woman acknowledges that even though she's read this passage countless times, she has overlooked these words: "Your generosity will result in thanksgiving to God."

She expounds: "If you're truly generous and not just giving to some cause, you don't care about getting credit. You do it because ultimately God gets all the credit. Generosity points people to God. I've always been timid about sharing my faith, but maybe being generous is another great way to share my faith."

Wow!

What's so great about this is that I'm not doing any "teaching." It's not like there's some financial expert showing us how Scripture tells us to give more to kingdom ministries. Rather, we're learning together. I try to limit the discussion of this passage to ten minutes, but it isn't working. Remember, these are entrepreneurs, business owners, and high-end money managers, all hungry to discuss these issues together.

Finally I click on another video, this time the story of Bishop Hannington, who felt God calling him to teach generosity to his people, despite the fact they lived with so little in a refugee camp in Uganda. It's a moving and inspiring story.

Something is happening. The wheels are turning. No one seems in a hurry to break for dinner, but Chris and Susan have arranged for us to head over to one of their favorite restaurants.

As the sun dips into the Gulf, we share a great meal, lively conversation, and laughter. We try not to talk about generosity but always do. Because it's beginning to feel like fun.

NINE

Priorities or Priority?

After a lovely dinner, we head back to Chris and Susan's place for the final session of the day. I've been to a lot of workshops and seminars throughout my career, and this is the point where people tend to go brain-dead. The after-dinner hour. Yawns come easily, despite your best efforts to stifle them. The temptation to go back to your room, flop down on the bed, and watch a ball game guarantees a few won't show up.

Not here.

Even during the breaks, everyone is so engaged. I don't take any credit for that because what I've learned is that Christians who have been blessed with wealth are hungry for this type of experience. They feel safe. They aren't embarrassed about their financial success. And they are with others who get it—who understand that having more than you need can be a blessing, but can also derail you from what you know is important.

By the time I pull up another video, all eyes are on the screen. This time, we listen to Jess and Angela Correll explain why they have chosen to give ten to twelve times the amount that they live on. Jess is a successful banker in Kentucky who freely admits that his biggest problem is greed. When he was eighteen, he and his seventeen-year-old brother decided they wanted to be the richest men in Kentucky and pursued that dream with abandon. They made a lot of money, but Jess soon discovered that more money doesn't make you happier or solve all your problems. In fact, he's pretty transparent about his shortcomings. Through a series of events in his life, including a divorce, which he blames on his singular focus on his business, he realized that the antidote to greed was what his father called "recklessly giving away money." His brother, Vince, who lost his battle with cancer in 1996, put it a little more graphically: "Money is like manure. If you let it stack up it starts to stink, but if you spread it around it can do a lot of good."

Once a year, Jess and Angela sit down and go over their strategic plan for their marriage, family, and giving. And they give themselves some pretty strict guidelines. Such as, "This year we will not acquire anything." They could easily spend a lot more money on themselves, but they have decided to spend more on others. And yet, they seem like the happiest people on earth. You don't come away feeling sorry for them because they give away so much. In fact, every time I watch this video, I experience a little envy. Apparently, I'm not the only one.

As soon as the video ends, one of the women turns to her husband and exclaims, "Hey, we should do that!"

"Whoa," came his honest, cautious response. And here's where I'm going to go out on a limb and share a generalization you may find unfair, even offensive.

Men tend to keep score with their money, whereas women tend to want security. When a wife feels they have enough to meet their needs, she's fine with giving the rest away. Her husband? Not so much. So to many men, setting your giving level at a multiple of what you spend on yourself doesn't make sense. This is likely true regardless of a person's financial status. I'm not as wealthy as the people in this JOG, but I tend to see money as a way to keep score—to let me know how I'm doing. That's why I can tend to be obsessive about building up my investments. It's my scorecard. My wife, Collynn, on the other hand, is far more open-handed than I am with our giving. If we have enough, she is eager to give wherever God leads us.

For the first time today, there's a little squirming going on, as well as a few knowing smiles. Guess who's squirming? Jim begins to explain why he responded the way he did to his wife's desire to change their giving formula.

"I look at our giving the same way I look at my business," he begins. "I need to look at the big picture and make decisions based on a lot of competing factors. I agree that we could be more generous, but we just need to be strategic about it."

All the guys in the room are nodding in agreement.

To be fair, I've heard women offer the same cautions about giving. In fact, most people default to the "let's not go overboard" position when it comes to how much they give away. Our human nature makes us quick to spend and slow to give. Why aren't we quick to give and slow to spend instead? We address this by taking a close look at a familiar passage of Scripture: Matthew 6:25-33. To refresh your memory, this is from the only sermon Jesus taught that is recorded in the Bible, what we often refer to as the Sermon on the Mount. And in this particular part of his sermon, Jesus zeroes in on an emotion that causes all of us to hold back when it comes to generosity: anxiety. It's what drives my efforts to make sure my savings account is healthy—what if the economy tanks, I lose my job, and I need to feed my family, pay the mortgage, put gas in the car? It's also what drives a guy to say "Whoa!" when his wife wants to quadruple their giving.

Do you remember the popular song from the 1980s, "Don't Worry, Be Happy"? In this sermon, Jesus explains how to actually live that way: "Don't worry. Put my kingdom first in your life and you will be happy." And few have unpacked this idea better than author Richard Foster in his book *Celebration of Discipline.* Foster explains that when we make God's kingdom our priority—seeking it above anything else—we experience a "joyful unconcern for possessions."[6] It's not that material wealth is bad; in fact, he says that often the people who have the least money love it the most. Complete trust in God produces freedom from the anxiety of not

---

[6] Richard J. Foster, *Celebration of Discipline: The Path to Spiritual Growth* (New York: HarperCollins, 1978), 87.

having enough. It's like that pivotal moment in my own life when I had to decide, "Do I believe God or not?"

I remember a few years ago having a conversation with a wealthy individual who decided to spend more money on others than on himself, adding, "Now my prayer is that my adult children will decide for themselves to do the same thing." It was the first time I had ever heard of such a thing, and it impressed me enough to make that my own prayer—that I would reach a point where I would give away more than I spent on myself. I'm not there yet, and that's okay. Remember, we're on a journey. Not everyone is going to arrive at the same destination, but what I love about these JOGs is how energized people get when introduced to a new paradigm. Here's another sampling of our discussion:

"As a businessman, the word 'reckless' isn't one of my favorites."

"It seems like the more successful we've been, the more I worry. There's just so much to manage."

"Isn't it interesting that we all look back when our lives were simpler, and for most of us, it was when we had very little."

The discussion is as rich as it is lively, and once again, I have to cut it off. It's been a long day, and we do our best to stick to our schedule. But first, I give them a homework assignment. Due tomorrow. Best-selling authors Randy Alcorn and Tim Keller have given us thirty questions to help us reflect on all that we've covered today. I ask them to spend some time going over the questions and selecting two that stand out to them. They don't have to answer the questions, just be willing to share why those questions caught their attention. Here are some samples:

- Does the thought of sacrificial generosity make me anxious because I feel I won't have enough to make ends meet?
- If an outsider were to look at how I use my time, my energy, and my resources, what would they learn about my priorities?
- What am I holding onto that's robbing me of present joy and future reward?
- Once they've finished college or are working on their own, would inheriting wealth help my children's eternal perspective or have a corrupting influence on their character, lifestyle, work ethic, or marriage?

Your first day of a JOG is just about over. All that's left is a little free time to take a walk on the beach, a dip in the pool, or just crash in your room. No one has asked you to increase your giving. No one has asked you about your current giving patterns. We've simply enjoyed a conversation about something pretty important to you. If you're like most who attend, your mind is swirling, but in a good way. You can't believe that you approached this JOG with a bit of dread, sort of the way you feel about going to the dentist. And it's been anything but dreadful. For the first time that you can remember, you were able to talk about money and God and giving and life without feeling guilty, without feeling like someone is trying to get something from you.

By tomorrow, you'll be back home (unless you decide to spend an extra day in Longboat Key for some fun and relaxation). Good night. God bless. And don't forget your homework.

TEN

Here It Comes

I don't know this for sure, but here are some conversations that I would bet at least a few couples have after they get back to their rooms for the night:

"So what did you think about today?" she asks.

"You first," he smiles.

"I loved it! And that surprises me because when Chris first talked to us about it, I was looking for an excuse not to attend."

"Really? Why's that? We've known Chris and Susan for a long time and like them a lot."

"It had nothing to do with Chris and Susan. It was the topic. When I heard the word 'generosity,' I knew that it really was going to be about money. But we didn't talk all that much about money, and when we did, it didn't bother me like it usually does. So, your turn—you seemed to be having a good time."

"I did, but it's not over. I have to admit, I feel a little

like I did that time when we were first married and got invited to a party—remember that?"

"You mean that time when they served us some nice snacks and then tried to sign us up to sell soap?"

"Ha—that's it exactly. I don't think Chris would do that, but I'll bet before we leave tomorrow, someone's going to ask us to write out a check."

Or maybe another couple has this "discussion":

"Oh, Jerry, wasn't this fun? I mean, seriously—it's been a long time since I've enjoyed myself as much as I did today. That story about the couple who capped their income so they could be generous? We oughta try that. Wouldn't it be fun to be able to buy a car for that young couple at church who's struggling? Or maybe offer to pay tuition for those two college students who plan to go to seminary? In fact, I've made a list of—"

"I *knew* that's what you were doing," he laughs. "But just remember, we've got our own kids who'll be going to college soon. And while things are going pretty well right now with my practice, who knows what the economy will be like next year. I'm all for being generous, but we need to be careful."

"I know, honey, but you've got to admit. Those people in the videos sure seem like they're having fun. Maybe we could just try it for a couple of months and see what happens."

"Maybe. I will say this. I've never been comfortable talking about things like this in a group, but today just seemed natural."

Okay, maybe they all just go back to their rooms and watch TV. But I doubt it, because everyone shows up the next morning, and once again, they jump right back into the conversation. Chris and Susan have set out a healthy spread of fruit, granola, yogurt, pastries, and fresh orange juice, along with coffee. As couples wander in, they grab something to eat and drink, and instead of talking about the weather or CNN's lead story, they talk about their homework. This, even before we officially get started, and here's why.

What we've learned from these JOGs is that people who love God and have been blessed with financial wealth really want to have a proper relationship with both. Yet they seldom feel safe or comfortable talking about these issues with others. So when it comes to money, they become protective and private about it. We get that, especially in today's environment where so much judgment and criticism have been hurled at the "one-percenters" (remember, we're almost *all* one-percenters in America). So we have worked very hard to create a safe place that respects the privacy people initially desire about money issues. We don't ask participants to share their net worth with us or each other. We never ask them to identify how much or what percentage of their income they give to the church or other charities. We don't whip out pictures of starving children and suggest that their increased giving could alleviate hunger. Why?

I'll answer with a question. If you were invited to spend twenty-four hours with a group of your wealthy friends and you knew that the goal was to raise more money for _____ (fill in the blank: missions, a new gymnasium for your church, church planting, urban ministry, etc.), how would you respond? Nothing against any effort to raise money for kingdom purposes, but that's not what we do. We create experiences where life-giving conversations like these can take place.

Here's another conversation I'm willing to bet at least one couple had on their way to breakfast:

"I wonder when it's going to come."

"What do you mean?"

"You know—the sales pitch. You don't really think they invited us here and paid for everything and they're not going to give us a pledge card, do you?"

"Hmm. I see what you mean. But it *has* been fun."

I start our first session of the day with a video about a couple who got a card from their church reminding them to get a gift for Pastor Appreciation Sunday. The wife was thinking about purchasing a $25 gift card, but the Lord had other ideas.

The couple discovered that their pastor and his wife really wanted to add to their family through adoption. Their only barrier was money.

"Remember how he shared with us how they are going through a Bible study to create a plan to get out of debt so they can adopt?" the husband asked. "They have $10,000 to go. Let's just pay off their debt."

This time it was the wife who said, "Whoa!" Though her husband had a good job, they had five kids, had expenses of their own, and were not really in a position to hand $10,000 over to someone.

"We can't just give money away like that," she protested.

"Why not?"

She agreed to pray about it and eventually embraced her husband's idea.

"I had plans to have some work done on our house and yard, but God showed me that while I was hoping to invest literally in the earth around my home, he wanted us to make an internal investment for his kingdom."

They visited their pastor and his wife and simply handed them a personal check for $10,000, adding, "Now don't act all weird around us, and whatever you do, don't tell anyone we did this."

Talk about a lively discussion. This idea of "random generosity" is unfamiliar to most in our JOG, at least at the $10,000 level.

"Shouldn't there be some sort of accountability, so you know they will use the money wisely?"

"But that might insult them because it suggests you don't trust them."

"I've paid for someone's groceries before, but that was like under fifty dollars. Still, the look on that young mother's face was worth every penny."

One guy sums up what a lot of us are thinking:

"I'm pretty careful about where I give. I want to make sure it's a ministry or organization that I agree with and that uses the money to help others, not just themselves. But I have to admit—watching that video makes me want to set aside some money to do something like they did."

What do *you* think?

We don't resolve the issue, because that's not why

we're here. The point of the video is not to encourage random acts of generosity, but to illustrate one of our foundational biblical truths: "It is more blessed (happy-making) to give than to receive." Generosity—whether carefully planned or randomly executed—always brings great joy to the giver, especially when we respond to the Holy Spirit's prompting. As illustrated by this line from the video: "The giving part of the story was fun, but the best part was to play a part in the secret plans of the God of the Universe."

Up to this point in a JOG, whatever is shared is done voluntarily. I don't recall ever having anyone sit mute through the discussions; even the occasional person who seems a little shy at first usually joins the conversation. But now it's time to discuss their homework—those thirty questions that Randy Alcorn and Tim Keller created for us. The assignment was to select two questions and be prepared to share your thoughts about them. Publicly. And if you recall, these are pretty tough questions. The kind that reach deep into your soul. So of course, I may have to sit through a little awkward silence, waiting for the first brave person to speak up.

Not exactly.

What I love about this assignment is hearing how people wrestle so honestly with questions about wealth, generosity, and faith. As I've observed before, Christians who love God and have been blessed financially really want to do the right thing when it comes to money. Perhaps more than the rest of us, they understand the power it has to deceive us into believing we are in control. Sometimes the thoughts expressed surprise the rest of us. For example, at this particular JOG, responding to the question, "Can I give radically to others even though they have brokenness and sin in their lives?" one of the men says something like this: "You know, I criticize liberals because they tend to want to just throw money at problems, but does that give me the right to be stingy?"

The cool thing is that he feels safe to say something that comes from his heart, even though it might seem out of character for him. How often do you feel safe enough to say what you're really thinking?

Before we break I hand out a simple form.

"Here it comes!" someone jokes.

Or maybe he's not joking. There's that old suspicion again. We get them all softened up and feeling generous and then hit them with the big ask.

Except we don't.

The form asks for their contact information, and we use that for only two purposes. One, we will notify them of any upcoming events—such as our annual Celebration of Generosity, which is like a JOG on steroids—and also e-mail them an electronic survey so they can let us know what they thought of their Journey of Generosity. Two, we will mail them a copy of Randy Alcorn's best-selling book, *The Treasure Principle*. We also give them the option of receiving a bimonthly e-mail from Generous Giving called *Storyline* that shares stories like the ones we've shown them during their JOG.

That's it—that is all they will hear from us. But we hope they keep listening.

Because if we listen, God will speak to us about generosity.

ELEVEN

If You Listen

When she was in high school, Renee Lockey decided she wanted to go into medicine. A good student, she pursued her dream, breezed through college, and entered medical school, eventually choosing to specialize in obstetrics and gynecology. To say she loved her job would be a huge understatement. And as a Christian, Renee viewed her career as a ministry.

"I'm blessed to walk with women and families through some really joyous times and also through some very challenging times," she explained. "I'm with that woman from the beginning of her pregnancy until when her baby takes its first breath."

By age thirty-seven, Renee had accomplished all she had set out to accomplish. She had a successful practice, had paid off all her debts, and enjoyed all that came with a comfortable salary. Life was exceedingly good for Renee.

"But something was missing," she said. "I wasn't in that place of contentment that I had imagined I would be at this point in my career."

And it wasn't just her. She worked in a large practice with other doctors and, of course, the requisite nurses you would expect in that setting.

"Over the years," Renee said, "I had observed that on average, the nurses were happier than the doctors, despite the fact that the doctors made a lot more money than the nurses, which enabled them to take nice vacations, drive the best cars, and seemingly never have to worry about paying the bills."

As she struggled to understand why her success as a doctor was not delivering what she thought it would, she went to a place where God had often spoken to her:

"It's when I lace up my running shoes and hit the trail that I hear really radical things from God. That's where I go to meet him. That's where he puts thoughts into my head that are beyond myself. That's where I get ideas."

It was on one of her runs that God spoke to her about money.

"You can't go to another culture without noticing what you have and what they don't have," she said about a recent missions trip she had taken to Haiti. "I realized that it's only by God's grace that I have anything more than they have—not that I'm entitled to it or earned it. He gave me the opportunities, the education, the funding—everything. It's like God was saying to me, 'What do you have that I haven't given you?'"

God said something else.

"I want you to work like a doctor and live like a nurse."

She did the math and it came out like this: to respond to God's invitation she would need to live on about one-fourth of her current salary. Renee considered how this would impact her life.

I'm not going to lie. It took some time to get used to living on a budget again. It had been quite a while since I had to even think about how I was spending my money. I also felt God was telling me to save less, something I was doing so I could retire at age fifty and still enjoy a comfortable lifestyle. But God wanted me to be able to share with others instead of spend and save so much for myself, and it was that act of obedience that filled that emptiness inside that I was experiencing. That hole in my life three years ago that I couldn't seem to fill is now filled to overflowing. By being able to be more generous, it not only has brought me greater joy, but it has given joy to others.

All because Dr. Renee Lockey listened.

If you attend a JOG, you might think the way we end it is unorthodox. Because in this final session we don't do anything. We don't try to resolve the questions that we've been addressing the past several hours. We don't suggest ways that you can be more generous. I have no predetermined outcome or goal that I hope to accomplish, as in "This JOG will be a success if the average giving for all who participated increases by ten percent."

Remember when I was back in college and made the

decision to believe that God is who he says he is and will do what he says he will do? That's how we end each JOG. By trusting God to privately speak to each person about what his or her next steps on the journey of generosity will look like. So I tell the group to go and listen for thirty minutes. To practice the discipline of silence so that they might hear from God. My instructions are simple:

- Ask the Holy Spirit to speak to you about this experience.
- Listen to what he may be saying to you.
- Write down one or more next steps in your giving journey and your journey with Jesus.
- If you are here as a couple, take the last ten minutes to share together.

Sounds easy, and for some it is. But for many, this is the hardest part of the JOG because we have this need to be doing something all the time. Especially for Type-A, hard-charging, success-oriented people. Our whole careers are oriented around action—fixing things, analyzing things, building things, setting and reaching goals. If we're lucky or feeling particularly religious, we might sit for a minute or two in complete silence, listening for some kind of sign from God. But if we're honest, that so-called quiet time gets pretty busy with reading, underlining, writing things down. Planning our next big God move. Doing nothing but listening for God to speak counters the way we otherwise live our lives—even our spiritual lives. If you think I'm exaggerating, stop right now, close the book, and try to sit in silence for five minutes. Don't make any plans. Don't let your mind wander to your job or your family. Just listen. Thirty minutes, even in our lovely beachside setting, seems like an eternity. Until God shows up. He always does.

Many who have attended a JOG identify this thirty-minute time of listening to be the most significant part of the weekend. It goes to the very heart of what we do: trust the Holy Spirit to speak rather than attempting to tell people what to do about generosity. If you've spent much time in church or with religious organizations, you know how hard it is for leaders to avoid giving answers. I recently met with the leader of a large ministry who had attended a JOG and wanted to adapt it for graduating Christian college students. I invited him to help us try that, but he expressed his hesitation, saying that his bias would be to tell the students what to think instead of allowing the Holy Spirit to direct them. It all goes back to trusting God and his word when he says, "Seek me first and I'll take care of all the other stuff" (Matthew 6:33, Todd's translation).

Even though I have facilitated more than one hundred of these JOGs, I follow my own instructions and listen for God's voice. Remember, this journey doesn't have a destination. You don't one day arrive at the perfect intersection of God and money. I need to—we all need to—listen to God regularly. Because as a guy who attended this JOG observed, this experience really isn't about money. It's not even about generosity. We may focus on these, but what we really do in our time together is learn about trust and faithfulness. Can we really trust God with our lives, and if so, how can we translate that trust into faithfulness with all of our resources—our time, our talent, and yes, our treasure?

It's not the thirty minutes that's important. It's the regular practice of asking God to speak to you, and then shutting everything out to listen for him. As the psalmist reminds us, "Be still before the Lord and wait patiently for him" (Psalm 37:7). So after talking together since we got here, we end in silence.

> *Then a great and powerful wind tore the mountains apart and shattered the rocks before the LORD, but the LORD was not in the wind. After the wind there was an earthquake, but the LORD was not in the earthquake. After the earthquake came a fire, but the LORD was not in the fire. And after the fire came a gentle whisper.*
> 1 Kings 19:11b-12

You have to be quiet to hear the whisper.

TWELVE

Join the Journey

What makes you happy?

Or maybe I should step back and ask a bigger question: Are you happy? Because according to a recent study, you might not be all that happy, despite the fact that you're likely making more money than ever. According to the World Happiness Report—yes, there really is such a thing—the United States, despite being one of the economically-richest countries in the world, only ranks #15 on the Happiness Scale.[7] And as our incomes have risen for the past fifty years, our well-being hasn't budged over that same period.

One of the editors of the report, Dr. Jeffrey Sachs of Columbia University, drilled down to try and determine what actually makes people happy. I'm not surprised by what he found, and you probably won't be either.

"People who are more generous, who express more

[7] See https://www.washingtonpost.com/news/inspired-life/wp/2015/05/11/why-many-americans-are-unhappy-even-when-incomes-are-rising-and-how-we-can-change-that/.

orientation toward others, more compassion, are also systematically reporting that they're happier," he writes.[8]

Isn't it ironic how so many Christians glibly quote the words of Jesus from the Book of Acts yet rarely apply them to the way they live?

"It is more blessed to give than to receive."

As I mentioned earlier, the word "blessed" from the Greek is accurately translated as "to make happy." Why do we need something like the World Happiness Report to show us we can trust Jesus?

Because of where you and I live, we have been assaulted by the exact opposite message: the road to happiness runs through financial independence. The higher your net worth, the happier you will be. As Christians, we inherently know that's a lie, but it's an appealing lie, one that can seem to be true. Especially when compared to other biblical truths that suggest we will be happier if we give it all away than if we hold onto it or acquire even more.

Which is why it's so important for you to join the conversation. I know that you don't believe the lie, but I also know how hard it is to trust the words of Jesus in our "culture of more." I also know that there are very few places where you feel safe enough to engage in an honest conversation about your wealth and your faith in Christ. We create that space for you, and our only goal is to encourage you to trust Jesus with these issues of wealth and faith. That's it. We don't offer five steps to greater joy or prescribe a formula that will make you happier. The only guarantee we offer is that if you ask Jesus to show

8 Ibid.

you what you can do with the blessings he has given you, he will show you. I know because I've seen it happen to so many people.

It happened to Tom and Bree Hsieh, who early in their marriage felt God telling them to live on the national median annual income, regardless of how much money they made. At the time, that number was around $45,000, so they settled in Pomona, California—the second largest suburb of Los Angeles, but also one of the poorest. The company Tom worked for, Earthlink, went public one day, and as Tom recalls, his stock options made him a millionaire several times over. By then they had discovered that God took care of them quite well on their $45,000 a year income, allowing them to experience the joy of generosity. So the next day, when his subordinates arrived at work in brand new Mercedes and high-end SUVs, he smiled to himself.

"I arrived at work in my 1991 Geo Metro. Three cylinders!" he said.

When I first heard Tom and Bree share their story, I thought they were crazy! Who lives like this? But then I got to hear their hearts and hear of the calling God has placed on their lives to live and serve in the inner city. They intentionally aligned their financial lives in order not to create distance between themselves and those they were seeking to serve. Most significantly, I heard of the joy and purpose they are experiencing in listening to and responding to God's invitation for their lives. (Search "Tom and Bree Generous Giving" on the web, or locate their video in our media library at generousgiving.org.)

We share these stories at our JOGs because they offer a compelling counter-argument to the predominant message of our culture. And they get people like you talking and thinking about what kind of story God has for you.

What's so cool about all of this is that in God's imagination, no two stories are alike. There's not "one way" to experience his joy through generosity. We leave that up to God because of that trust thing. He is who he says he is, he does what he promises, and if you listen he will guide you into more happiness, joy, and purpose than you've ever experienced.

So what's the ask? Why have we given you this book? We want you to join the journey, and you can do that in several different ways.

First, consider hosting a Journey of Generosity—or JOG—for twelve to sixteen of your friends who might benefit from it. People like you who love God and have been blessed financially. Invite people you enjoy because a JOG really is fun. As a host, you will provide a comfortable environment for an overnight experience. This could be your home, a hotel downtown, a B&B, a vacation place, or a resort. Use your imagination. Ask yourself, "What would be a really cool place where I can invite some friends to hang out with us?"

As the host, your responsibility is to provide a comfortable environment at no charge to your friends. All they have to do is get there. You don't have to be a Bible scholar or have this topic of generosity all figured out. We at Generous Giving provide a facilitator and all the materials for the JOG at no charge, including an invitation that explains a JOG to the friends you plan to invite. And to help you along the way, we provide you with a JOG "Concierge" who will be available to answer any questions as you prepare for your JOG. It's that simple—you host, we facilitate, and everyone has a great time. If that appeals to you, let me know by using the contact information at the end of the book. By hosting a JOG, you will help start a new conversation for change in individual lives, your community, and the world. Seventy-eight percent of those who have attended a JOG report a change in perspective or practice as a result of the event. And those who have hosted rate the investment of their time and money as a 9.7 out of 10.

Second, you could attend a Journey of Generosity Facilitator Training. If what you've read here resonates with your sense of calling, we'd be thrilled to have you join the team as a volunteer facilitator. We have trained hundreds of people to facilitate these conversations with their friends, boards they serve on, and churches they attend. In fact, one of the most gratifying aspects of our work is to observe others facilitating these life-giving conversations. Our volunteers consistently report facilitating these experiences as one of the most satisfying ministry opportunities in which they participate.

Third, I'd love to have you join about five hundred others at our annual "Celebration of Generosity." As I described it earlier, it's like a JOG but on a much larger scale. It is quite remarkable to be in a room filled with hundreds of generous people. What can you expect at this event? Great music from well-known recording artists. Challenging messages from Christian leaders such as Randy Alcorn, Tim Keller, Lysa TerKeurst, Mark Batterson, Chip Ingram, Nancy Leigh DeMoss, John Ortberg, Rick Warren, and Henry Blackaby. A lot of really good food. Free time to enjoy the surroundings (we're pretty good at finding fun places). And live, in-the-flesh stories like the ones I've shared throughout this book. You'll get to meet these inspiring people, ask them questions, see if they're for real or not (they are). And you will also meet and rub shoulders with others just like you who are at various stages on the journey. These annual events begin on a Thursday afternoon and conclude after a late-morning brunch on Saturday.

Everyone wants "more than enough." That's the essence of abundance. Before credit cards, you wanted to make sure you had more than enough cash in your wallet before you took your family to dinner. Credit cards now satisfy that inherent desire to have more than we need. If you're fortunate to have acquired significant wealth, you likely have more than enough yet realize deep down in your heart that there's something more out there. And there is. When we surrender everything we have to God, he rewards us with the abundant life of joy, peace, purpose, and fulfillment. That's the more that I believe God implanted on our spiritual DNA, and it's yours to experience. Not somewhere off in the future, but now.

I began this book by confessing how much I loved money. I still like it, but my perspective on it has completely changed. Much of that learning has come from observing and serving those who have a lot more of it than I do.

What I've learned is that money doesn't make you happy, but sharing it does. It truly is more blessed (happy-making) to give than to receive. In fact, in the past twenty years, I've never met an unhappy generous person, nor have I ever met a former giver! Now we have the incredible privilege of helping to facilitate conversations that are spreading throughout God's kingdom, and I'd love to have you join us.

To explore any of these three opportunities, reach out
to our JOG Concierge
at
Concierge@generousgiving.org
or
visit our website for more information:
generousgiving.org

WHAT PEOPLE HAVE SAID ABOUT THEIR JOG EXPERIENCES

"I have always viewed generosity as an issue of obedience. I came away from the JOG feeling as though generosity is something I've been invited into, and it is the key to unlock the door to a full, adventurous, and abundant life."

"We greatly enjoyed our JOG retreat. One of our discoveries at the JOG was that we both wanted to do more Spirit-led giving, that when a need was discovered/presented we would respond right then. That was on Saturday, and on Sunday at church we saw a couple in our Sunday school class who looked downcast. Sally asked what was happening, and they shared quietly that due to medical bills and a failed business, they were losing their home. My wife, Sally, and I looked at each other, both nodded yes, and wrote them a check on the spot. We have experienced the greatest joy in giving this gift."

"It's a completely new perspective. It makes my head spin. It's irrationally beautiful."

"Listening for what God would say to us has been a recent theme in our lives, and it began at this event."

"We felt like we were pretty generous going into this. I think what we left with was the encouragement to trust God even more in being generous."

"The JOG was perfect timing for my wife and me. We had been praying about finding Christian peers who desire to do more with their wealth than just exist or save for a rainy day, people who desire to rise to another level of giving."

"The weekend was biblically based as well as being very practical."

"Generosity is possible regardless of your economic situation. I plan to spread this message throughout my sphere of influence."

"We decided to give out of capital in addition to income because of the JOG. This doubled our giving last year."

"We as a couple have decided to pray about our giving together, and to go about it with a purposeful Christian perspective. We are being more generous and free about giving in ways we didn't even think about before."

"Prior to my Journey of Generosity, I was a faithful tither and supporter/gift giver as I felt inspired or moved to give. Now, as a family, we are changing everything in our lives to respond to God's grace with great generosity, beyond the notion that a tithe is sufficient."

"The JOG was an incredible experience for us as a couple! We loved our group and have already met for dinner and plan to continue meeting. It encourages us to be around others who are generous and intentional!"

"I was quite surprised to receive an invitation to participate. I've had several business setbacks and thought the purpose of the event was to shake down high net worth Christian businessmen who may be holding on to their money too tight. Little did I know that in God's economy, net worth and value are not measured in dollars. My definition of giving and what God is directing me to give was totally redefined. Because my financial giving lacked a few zeros made me feel insecure and guilty and less of a Christian. My time, my pain, my humility, my fears, my setbacks, and my failures are to be shared and "given" away. I'm still learning that I've always been poor, yet rich in God's grace. I've been emptied of "me," so the only thing I can give is the gift inside of me . . . Jesus Christ."

"Thanks to JOG, I feel that I understand the gospel more and my heart feels more free to live from grace."

ABOUT THE AUTHOR

 As a founder of Generous Giving, Todd has been actively engaged in spreading the biblical message of generosity for twenty years. In his current role as president, Todd acts as a key spokesperson, relating with givers and implementing strategies for advancing the generosity message. He holds a bachelor's degree in economics and entrepreneurship from Baylor University and spent eleven years with Campus Crusade for Christ International (Cru), where he served in Russia, Yugoslavia, and in the United States. Prior to joining Generous Giving, Todd was a partner in an investment management firm, advising high net worth clients on growing and using wealth wisely. Todd's passion is to disciple others, and given his experience in ministry leadership, major donor development, and philanthropic advising, he is particularly suited to encourage Christians to excel in the grace of giving. He and his wife, Collynn, have five children and live in Orlando, Florida.